The Meaning of Contraception

alba house ▪ DIVISION OF THE SOCIETY OF ST. PAUL
STATEN ISLAND, N. Y. 10314

The Meaning of Contraception

By Mary Rosera Joyce

Nihil Obstat:
Daniel V. Flynn, J.C.D.
Censor Librorum

Imprimatur:
Joseph P. O'Brien, S.T.D.
Vicar General, Archdiocese of New York
December 20, 1969

Library of Congress Catalog Card Number 75-110591

SBN: 8189-0165-9

Designed, printed and bound in the U.S.A. by the Pauline Fathers and Brothers, 2187 Victory Blvd., Staten Island, N.Y. 10314 as part of their communications apostolate.

176
J89m
148083

TO ALL THOSE WHO DEEPLY LOVE

THE EARTH AS THEIR HOME

IN THE UNIVERSE

PREFACE

In the months before *Humanae Vitae* was published, it seemed that most Catholics and the Christian people in general expected a change in the Papal teaching on contraception. A friend of mine said, "The handwriting is on the wall!" During this period of uncertainty when many were forming their own consciences, my work on the meaning of contraception was undertaken. And it was completed about two months before Pope Paul made his decision known to the people.

This book was written, then, in a most ambiguous situation. Without strong motivation I would not have been able to sustain the intensive effort involved in its composition. But it seemed to me a way of expressing convictions that were based on my own intuition, reason and faith, and that were encouraged by the document of Vatican II on marriage.

After *Humanae Vitae*, some adjustments by way of references were made in the manuscript in order to relate it to the encyclical. But no change in the substance of the book, or in its principles, was made. However, I felt that similar conclusions in the encyclical still demanded much more explanation than was given within the short space of the document itself.

There are many writers to whom I am indebted for their personal views on contraception, most of them critical of the traditional reasons for declaring it immoral. Some of these writers are Dr. John Rock, John T. Noonan, G. Egner, Louis Dupre, Germain Grisez, Louis Janssens, Rosemary Reuther, Sidney Callahan, Michael Novak, Dietrich von Hildebrand and others. But my own thinking has been most deeply influenced, though indirectly so, by Heidegger, Buber, Marcel, Maritain,

Teilhard, Montessori, Jung, Frankl and many others.

Also I wish to express thanks to Rev. Paul Marx, O.S.B., of St. John's University, Collegeville, Minnesota for the considerable amount of material, mainly in the form of articles, which he sent to me, as well as for our correspondence on the subject. Most of all, I am grateful to Bob, my husband, for sharing my convictions and for his personal influence in the development of this work.

Mary Rosera Joyce
January 1, 1970

CONTENTS

INTRODUCTION

After a long waiting in the midst of agitated controversy, Pope Paul's encyclical on Human Life appeared to be a totally conservative statement. But many people were surprised by the radical nature of his firmness and courage. A profound rootedness, a strong and genuine intuition, underlay his apparently conservative stand. In order to understand the encyclical, this intuition must be explored and articulated more fully.

That it is an intuition both of faith and of reason appears in the two basic principles on which the conclusions of the encyclical are based. In the area of faith, Pope Paul pointed out that marriage, as a sacrament, signifies the union of Christ and the Church. And in the area of reason, he upheld the "inseparable connection" between the unitive and the procreative meanings of the conjugal act. The relationship between these principles of faith and reason is rich for thoughful study and growing insight.

By saying that "the men of our day are especially capable of perceiving the deeply reasonable and human character" of the inseparable relation between the two meanings of the conjugal act, Pope Paul hardly means that the people of our day are actually now understanding this relation, but that they are capable of doing so. Such an understanding requires faith, good will and the ability for thinking in depth. When he talks of the "laws inscribed in the very being of man and of woman," Pope Paul is inviting a kind of thinking that departs from the usual biological and psychological views of morality in marriage. It is important that he pointed to the very *being* of man and of woman as the basis for the inseparable relation of the two meanings of the conjugal act. The unity of the person's being resists any deep forms of separatism, even if done in a single act. But this principle of inseparability in the being of man and of woman seems esoteric or incomprehensible to many, including philosophers and theologians. Its largely intuitive nature seems to escape their grasp.

Yet the recent tendency to think that the natural law should be obvious to everyone, if it really is a *natural* law, blocks any readiness for in-depth thinking on the subject. It is obvious to all men that they need food to live. But the natural law is the law of a person's entire nature and being. And no one is ready to hold that the nature of the human person is easy to understand, or that it is obvious to anyone. Apparently the natural law was not obvious to the Chosen People if it had to be revealed to them by God through Moses in most of the ten commandments, and it was only partly revealed at that time. Without the light of revelation man can see only his fallen nature through a darkened intellect. Divine grace and revelation help him to see his *nature* as it is meant to be, and they act as powerfully therapeutic agents in healing his nature of its deformities. Grace and revelation strengthen in man his natural intuition of being. Thus, the intuition of being, our natural access to knowledge of the natural law, must not be abandoned. It is the greatest need of our time. There can be no authentic theology or Christian morality without beingful thinking.

Through a clear recognition of the original source of judgment in intuition, a thinker exposes to himself the very roots of his mind in reality, and experiences the tremendous challenge of intuitive knowledge to his powers for articulation and communication. A similar, though less intense, condition of mind is experienced by almost every person, and is commonly expressed in the words, "I know it but cannot say it." Often, we think we know something with certainty and clarity until we are called upon to say what it is, or until we are forced to defend what we know. The Christian religion, richly grounded in the great

mysteries of being, is full of such intuitions. Truths that are
strongly and deeply known often are not articulated at all, or
when reasons are put forth in statements, the effect is faltering
and inadequate. But faith seeks understanding, and intuitions
of being seek articulation. In times of crisis and confusion, this
need is most deeply felt.

Like the human embryo rooted in the mother, the human
mind intuitively rooted in the ground of being grows by being
differentiated in many complex and interrelated structures. If
the embryonic person is not developed in the womb, death or
severe retardation result. Yet, we seem much less aware of the
lack of development and the consequent retardation in our
mental lives.

Just as a child cannot be born as an undeveloped mass of
protoplasm and be expected to live, an undeveloped awareness
of our sexuality leaves us unprepared for life. But many people
react to a closely reasoned study of sex. They tend to regard
fine distinctions as useless hair-splitting or as mental gymnastics
and semantic exercises that are far removed from the experience
of living. But these refined distinctions are really the result of
thinking at jeweler's range. A jeweler who studies a ruby or
diamond under a high-powered microscope refines his perception
of the precious stone. This kind of high-powered concentration is
required if we are to differentiate our awareness of any area of
reality, including that of human sexuality. Without such a re-
finement of understanding, the spontaneity of love and sex
must remain in a grossly primitive state.

In trying to discover and express the meaning of a form
of sexual behavior such as contraception, definition is an important beginning. And much depends upon the adequacy of
this beginning. Though meanings are more fully revealed in
descriptions and analogies than in definitions, these must be
guided by definition. Besides having a propensity for identifying
things that are not identical, and for separating things that are

not separate, the undifferentiated mind has a great propensity for poor comparisons. Analogies must be used with careful discernment, otherwise they are as effective in producing erroneous judgments as they are in revealing true meanings and values.

Though this study of contraception begins with its definition, followed by a descriptive analysis of faulty and revealing analogies, the meaning that is gradually revealed is based on a metaphysics of man's being and sexuality. Not until the central chapters of the book is this foundation made explicit. Thereafter, it becomes possible to develop, in and through their grounding in being, the theological and moral dimensions of the meaning of contraception.

The main point of this book is that the principle of inseparability in human actions is based on *being* rather than on *biology*. Meaning and morality that are based on being are radical, in the sense of being deeply rooted, rather than liberal or conservative. Though these latter categories seem so freely applied to Christians today, they are not truly Christian designations. Christ was neither a liberal nor a conservative. He was, and remains, radical in the best sense of that word; one who came not to destroy, but to fulfill and to surpass, the law. The same is true of John, the voice of one crying in the wilderness to prepare the way. When Jesus asked his disciples about John, whether they had gone into the desert to see a reed shaken in the wind (Luke 7-24), he was implying that John was a radical man, one too deeply rooted in being to be swayed by anything. We see that the trees in our own environment, if they are not to be toppled in a storm, must be deeply and expansively rooted in the ground. And we know from what we see and understand about these things, that the same is true for human minds and hearts.

Chapter 1

A DEFINITION OF CONTRACEPTION

Contraception may be defined as the internal separation of the coital act from its generative power. In this definition, the words — nature, artificial, frustration, purpose and interference — are avoided. Words such as biological, physical and physiological are omitted. At this time in the history of thought on the subject, a good definition will transcend these words and their meanings. Instead of helping to clarify the meaning of contraception, they tend to create or increase confusion.

First of all, contraception is a separation. Something that would be united without the use of contraceptives is separated by them. A human personal action is separated from one of its fully human powers.

Secondly, the separation is internal rather than external because the unity of the coital act and its generative power is broken from within.

Because contraception is defined as a separation that is internal to the relation of the coital act and its generative power, the regulation of conception by periodic continence is excluded from the definition of contraception. Conception-regulation by periodic continence is not a separation of the coital act from its generative power, much less an internal separation. As will be shown later, the relation of the act to its power is sustained by this method, and is actually assimilated into human knowledge and self regulation. Though continence and contraception may be used for the same purpose: controlling conception, this same purpose does not make them identical. Two men who have the same purpose in working for a living may do very different things. Because they are both done for the salary, the work of a teacher and the work of a butcher are not the same thing.

Finally, the realities that are internally separated by contraception, the personal action of coital union and the person's generative power, must be considered as part of the definition. The expression "generative power" is used instead of "reproductive power" because "reproduction" is an agricultural term more appropriate for plants and animals than for man. The expression "generative power" is also preferred to "procreative power" since the meaning of "procreation" tends to include the nurture and education of the child as well as the beginning of his life. The generative power is the power to co-create, to bring into existence, together with another person, and with God and nature, a new human person.

In this definition of contraception, nothing is said about biological organs, purpose of organs, purpose of acts, or biological nature and the nature of a human act. Nothing more nor less is said than that a human personal action is internally separated from one of its powers. Nothing is said about the moral status of the reality being defined.

So that the definition may lead gradually to a fuller understanding of the meaning of contraception, inquiries into the nature of the coital act and its generative power, and into the relationship that exists between the act and its power, are required. The meaning of contraception as a separation is implied in the meaning of these elements of the definition.

In previous times, the coital act was thought to be a physical or biological act, probably because copulation was viewed as something that man has in common with animals. Even Sigmund Freud, the father of modern psychology, viewed human sexual energy as a physiological force that deeply affects psychic life. And there are contemporary writers who interpret the sexual difference between man and woman as a difference in anatomy only, with the implication that sex is only a biological reality. However, at the same time, it is being ardently denied that coital union of persons is only a biological act. More and more, despite the insight-lag about the nature of human sexuality, coital intercourse is being regarded as an act of the whole person, a freely willed expression of intelligence and love, as well as a complete involvement of the physical dimension of the person's reality. But this sexual act may be, and often is, separated from the power to love, and from other powers in which its human value is deeply rooted. An example of a separation of sex from love is the *Playboy* ideology and practice.

In previous times, and still today, the human generative power is thought to be nothing more than a biological function. The biblical command to increase and multiply is being called a biological imperative. But the generative power of the human person is essentially different from other biological powers such as the circulatory and respiratory powers. In the science of biology, the reproductive system is classified along with, and on the same level as, the circulatory, respiratory and other physiological systems. This classification is adequate for animals, but inadequate for human beings. In the human person, as in animals, the powers of circulation and respiration are activated without personal choice and behavior. But the generative power is activated only through personally chosen behavior.

The human *organs* of generation may be viewed as biological, but the *power* of generation is much more than biological. It is a power of the whole person through his freely chosen action. Through the human generative power, other *persons* come into existence. And they come into existence, not primarily by means of a sub-personal biology, but primarily, by a personally chosen action. Even exceptions to the voluntary nature of this personal act, such as the copulative act of a psychotic, or the forceful coercion of a rapist, are not simply biological events; they are psychological events as well.

In order to understand the human generative power more adequately, the real distinction between powers and organs must be clearly realized. Unless this distinction is understood, the human generative power, which is much more than biological will be falsely identified with the biological nature of the generative organs.

By way of example, the organs of speech are biological in nature, but the power to speak is primarily mental in nature. The organ of speech is that *through which* the power to speak is actualized. Furthermore, when an organ of vision is impaired, the physician does not think that the power of vision is also impaired, otherwise he would not think it useful to transplant another organ so that the power to see may be activated again. The power cannot be activated without the organ, nor the organ without the power. The organ and the power are internally related, though they are not at all identical.

There are many examples, other than that of speech, in which the relation of a power to its organ transcends biology in the human person. The hands are biological organs, but the power to play the piano, while it is partly biological, is primarily mental, emotional and artistic in nature. Any use of the hands for such things as sewing, typing, building, etc., is done by a power that is much more than biological. Instances of extra-sensory perception witness to the trans-biological nature of the power to perceive. And the real difference between the organ of thinking, the brain, and the power to think, shows the falsity of identifying a human power with the biological nature of its organ.

Other examples of the essential difference between a power and its organ appear in the human acts of listening and observing. In these examples, there is a difference not only between a power and its organ, but also between involuntary and voluntary activations of a power. Hearing and seeing may be involuntary, but listening and observing are personally chosen actions.

Through its biological organ, the ear, the power to hear may be activated by any sound, but the person may not be aware of what is heard. The power to give attention to sounds, or to listen, is a power for a personally chosen action. Similarly, a person may see something and be unaware of what he is seeing. There are things we see everyday that we would be unable to describe if someone asked for a description. However, when we give our attention to something that we see, or when we observe it, the biological organs of vision are assimilated within a personally chosen action. The power to observe, though it cannot be activated without the organs of vision, cannot be activated without personal choice.

Hearing and seeing may be called biological movements in the auditory and optical organs. Similarly, involuntary movements in the organs of generation, such as the generation and involuntary releasing of sperm, and the movements of ovulation and menstruation, may be called biological movements of the generative power. But human generation, like listening and observing, cannot take place without personal, voluntary action. The power to generate new persons, though partly biological, like the powers to listen and to observe, is much more than biological. All of these powers are personal, in the fullest sense of the word *person*-al.

But there is, also, an essential difference between the powers to listen and observe, and the power of generation. The first two can be activated by the individual person himself. But the generative power can be activated only together with another person; *it is specifically an interpersonal power*. Because the generative power is activated only through the personally chosen action of another person, including factors of agreement and disagreement, it is even more trans-biological than the powers to listen and observe.

Even those powers that are activated without voluntary, personal choice, are powers of the person. For example, it is not the power of vision, nor the organ of vision that sees; it is the person who sees. And the *entire* person sees through his eyes. It is not the ears that hear, but the person who hears. Similarly, it is not the organs of generation that form and release sperm, that ovulate and menstruate; it is the person who ovulates, or who does any of these things, involuntary though they be. And with additional personal meaning, it is the person who listens and observes, or who, together with another person, generates new human life. Every activation of the generative power is imputed not to a biological process, but to an interpersonal action, just as every activation of the powers to listen and observe is imputed not to a biological process, but to a personal action.

What, then, is the relationship between the coital act and its generative power?

For centuries, the relationship was thought to be one more or less of *identity*. Coitus was thought to exist primarily, if not totally, for the purpose of generation, and was justified by conception and birth. More than likely, this was due to the manner in which man was defined as an animal, differing from other animals by being rational, but being basically an animal nevertheless. Since the copulation of animals exists mainly for the purpose of reproduction, and since the coitus of persons was strongly identified with the biological purpose of sex in animals, it was readily thought that coitus and reproduction are practically identified in meaning.

More recently, the relationship of the coital act to its generative power is thought to be one of *separation*. Since it is now known that most coital acts are not actually generative by nature, it is thought that the coital act and its generative power are separate realities that are only externally united. In the sense that the coital act must be performed in order to fulfill the desire for a child, the act and the power are admitted to have a kind of unity, but an external, rather than internal, unity. The coital act and its generative power would then be united in a way similar to that of a writing tool and a piece of paper when a letter is being written. In order to write the letter, a writing instrument is necessary, but the instrument and the paper, though they are externally united while the writing is being done, are really separate things.

The paper and the pencil, however, are not internal parts of a whole being greater than themselves. The coital act and its generative power, on the other hand, are parts of a totality in which all parts are internally united with all other parts. This totality is the human person. The internal parts of a whole are internally and intrinsically united with one another. Thus, the brain is internally present in the hands and feet, not spatially but ontologically. Due to the intrinsic unity of the human person in all his parts, no human power is only externally or extrinsically united with the personal action through which that power is activated.

In considering the relationship of the coital act to its generative power, we see that the coital act does not necessarily activate its generative power, but that the coital act is necessary if the generative power is to be activated. From the point of view of the generative power, there is necessity in the relationship, but not from the point of view of the coital act. This lack of necessity in the relationship, from the point of view of the coital act, seems to argue against an internal unity of the coital act with its generative power. But there is necessity in the relationship, from the point of view of the generative power, and necessity of a specifically *personal* kind. The generative power is internally structured in the voluntary interpersonal power for the coital act. In fact, part of the meaning of the generative power is the person's power for the coital act. Through its internal structuring in the power for the coital act, the generative power is internally present in the coital act itself.

If this is so, why is the generative power not necessarily

activated by the coital act? In the majority of cases, the coital act is not generative. But must it be supposed, that if there is an internal unity of the generative power with the coital act, every act would be generative? Does internal or intrinsic unity imply some kind of identity?

An example may help to show that the internal unity of parts in a whole does not imply identity of parts, nor a one-to-one relationship between a human act and one of its powers.

The relationship between the fingers and the main part of the hand is one of internal unity. These parts are not just externally united as a glove and hand when the hand is gloved. But, in the mutually internal unity of parts that exists in the hand, there is no identity. The whole hand may be moved without specifically moving the fingers. Likewise, the hand may be moved while specifically moving the fingers, as in typing or playing the piano. While being internally united, the fingers and hand are really distinct from each other. But this real distinction does not imply a separateness of fingers and hand any more than it implies their identity.

Just as it is impossible to move the fingers without moving the internal muscles of the hand, it is impossible to generate new human life without coital intercourse (or some kind of personally chosen action such as artificial insemination). But it is possible to act in coital union without activating the generative power, just as it is possible to move the hand at the wrist without specifically moving the fingers. Similarly, coitus without the generation of new life is no evidence against the mutually internal unity of the generative power and the coital act.

Contraception, then, is an internal separation of an interpersonal action of coital union from the fully human generative power that is internally structured in this action by the unity of the person's being. It is a separation of an interpersonally chosen action from one of its interpersonal powers, each of which is internal to the other.

By different ways of separating the organs of generation from the generative power, by chemical or mechanical means, contraception is effected. Sterilization is definable exactly as contraception, but is done by surgical means. As all human biological organs are distinct from the powers they express, the organs of generation are distinct from the generative power. But this real distinctness of powers and organs, while not being an identity between them, is not a separation either. There is a mutually internal unity between human powers and the organs in which these powers are expressed.

But contraception is something more than separating the *organs* of generation from the generative *power*. The separation of the organ from its power is a means to the essential separation of contraception, that is, the separation of an interpersonally chosen *action* from a *power* internally structured in this action.

Chapter 2

INTERFERENCE WITH NATURE CLARIFIED

Only after contraception is defined apart from any question of nature, or interference with nature, is it wise to discuss its meaning as an interference with nature. First of all, the meaning of *nature*, in relation to contraception, must be accurately differentiated.

The downward plunge of a waterfall, the falling of rain and the growing of grass are movements of nature. When the water is diverted from the precipice to prevent the waterfall, or when an umbrella is used to divert the fall of rain, or when a lawnmover is used to cut grass, these are all interferences with nature. Man cannot live without interfering with nature. Plowing the soil, sowing seeds in rows, harvesting crops and storing them are interferences with nature that would not exist if man did not inhabit the earth. Instead of eating it raw, man cooks his meat. He cuts down trees, saws and hammers the wood to build himself a house. We must say then, that it is natural for man to interfere with nature.

But, where he has no moral qualms about killing animals for food, man has grave moral reservations about killing other persons for food. Where he has not thought twice about sterilizing animals, he is reluctant to sterilize himself. Where cosmological and biological movements of nature can be made to serve his purposes, man has a need to interfere with nature. But when he is confronted with the nature of a person, *interference* is changed in meaning, even as *nature* is changed in meaning.

The reproductive system in animals is simply biological, but in man, it is personal as well as biological. Even the digestive system in man is not simply biological. Because his biology is that of a person, there is nothing in man that is simply biological in nature. The heart of a man is a personal organ of circulation, as well as a biological organ. But the heart of an animal is not personal at all. Therefore, it is quite a different matter to interfere with the circulatory system of an animal, to shoot it in the heart so that its flesh may be eaten as food, than to interfere in a similar way with the circulatory system of a human person.

The meaning of personal nature is to be clearly distinguished from biological nature in animals and plants, and from cosmological nature in minerals, water, earth, wind, fire and rain. Interferences with a personal movement of nature, such as contraceptive interference, have a very special meaning. When contraception is described as an interference with nature, the meaning of nature is radically different from biological and cosmological meanings of nature.

When a man interferes with his own personal nature, he is doing something significantly different from interfering with biological or cosmological nature. For this reason, the expression "laws of nature" and the expression "natural law" are really distinct, though not separate, in meaning. *Laws of nature* are cosmological and biological laws, and belong to the dimension of nature that is subject to human interference. But the *natural law* is the law of a very special kind of nature; it is the law of a person's nature. And everything in the human person, from his liver and pancreas to his feelings and thoughts belong to his person-nature. *In the person-nature of a human being, the laws of nature are assimilated within and transformed by the natural law.*

In plants and animals, the laws of nature are radically other than the natural law. But in human persons, the bio-physical laws of nature are profoundly internal to the natural law. In the internal unity of the human person, the laws of nature are subsumed within, humanized and personalized by, the natural law. In the human person, these laws are distinct but never separate.

Thus, a man falls from a cliff by a law of nature, but this law of nature is personalized in his being. Even though they fall at the same rate of speed, the fall of a man and the fall of a rock are essentially different events.

Ethical imperatives of the natural law are not derived from the laws of nature, nor from cosmological or biological principles, but from the person-nature of the human being in his voluntary behavior — a nature that includes, while greatly transcending the laws of nature. This is why the reproductive system of animals is subject to the laws of nature, whereas the generative system of man is fully subject to the natural law, as are all his other partly biological systems.

The nature of man is the nature of a person, not the nature of a body, nor of bodily organs. Nor is it the nature of a spirit. The person is a total being who is present in each part of himself. The person is present in each one of his fingers and in his digestive system, as much as in his thoughts and feelings. A person's smallest finger is worthy of the same respect and reverence as is the person himself. Since there is a special importance in the nature of a person, actions toward one's own person and toward the person of others must be guided by the natural law. And this natural law is precisely the imperative of unity that originates in the depths of the person's *being*.

This does not mean, however, that the person must not interfere with his nature in any way. When he shaves his beard, cuts his hair, cuts his fingernails and toenails, or when he bathes to wash away perspiration, he is interfering with something in his nature. But fingernails and hair are not vital organs, nor even living tissues. One must distinguish, then, between an *accidental* interference with his nature, as in the above examples, and an *essential* interference with his nature.

Hair is meant to be cut in order to be groomed, fingernails are meant to be trimmed, and perspiration is meant to be washed away in a bath. Good grooming and cleanliness are as much a manifestation of the person's nature as wearing clothes and shoes, and eating with table utensils. In all of these things, the fundamental difference of the human person from animals is evident. But in none of these things is he separating one of his personally chosen actions from a power or movement of his nature internally structured in this action. Such an interference with his nature would be a matter of a different kind, an essential rather than an accidental interference.

Chapter 3

COMPARISONS WITH DIETING

The use of diet pills would constitute a separation of the human act of eating food from the digestive power internally structured in this action if the pills worked by putting the digestive power out of action. However, many of these pills act by lessening the appetite for food. When a human appetite is compulsive, or when it results in disorders such as those following upon overeating and alcoholism, drugs that reduce the appetite would be aids to health. But the amphetamines that reduce the appetite for food often have harmful effects. Generally, they produce insomnia, and must be accompanied by sleeping pills. Hypertension, nervousness, emotional tension, hallucinations and excessively rapid beating of the heart can result from misuse. Other diet pills are digestives, diuretics, metabolic stimulants, laxatives and bile modifiers. Drugs that modify, slow down or speed up natural processes without putting them even temporarily out of action are not necessarily *essential* interferences with the person's nature. But if they produce disorders in the person, they are essential interferences with his nature.

Drugs taken to slow down or speed up the natural process of ovulation are clearly distinguishable from those that put this process even temporarily out of action. Also, if there were pills available for lessening a compulsive or overactive sex appetite, these would be essentially different in meaning than the anovulant pills that separate a personally chosen action from a power internally structured in this action.

Other comparisons of sexual activity with eating and chewing have been tried. Diet control by eating low calorie food has been thought by some to be an interference with nature that is comparable to contraception. But eating low calorie foods is not an internal separation of the human act of eating from the digestive power structured in this act. The digestive power continues to function. Chewing gum, and stimulating the flow of saliva without providing the food toward which saliva is directed, has been viewed as an interference with nature similar to contraception. But if comparisons are to be made, the act of chewing and stimulating the flow of saliva without food to be digested is much more comparable to the coital act and stimulating the release of semen when the generative power is naturally unactivated.

All comparisons between the act of eating and the coital act, and between modifications and interferences with these acts, are weak and misleading. Though it may be motivated by psychic needs, eating food is basically motivated by a biological necessity of a personal kind. But the coital act is least meaningful when biologically motivated. Whereas the coital act is essentially interpersonal, needing to be integrated into a total way of life with another person in marriage, as well as being fruitful in the conception and birth of new human persons, the act of eating, even though it may be accompanied by the fellowship of others, is a good for the individual person himself. It is not essentially interpersonal in nature. Eating is much simpler in meaning than the coital act, and is not bound up with lifelong commitments to, and responsibilities for, *other* persons. But the greatest difference of all is the way in which the act of eating is primarily based in a physiological necessity, and the coital act in freedom and interpersonal love. Analogies of sex with eating should be avoided. Since the coital act is one of interpersonal communication, it is much more appropriate to compare it with another act of interpersonal communication. The will be done in chapter six.

Chapter 4

COMPARISONS WITH THERAPEUTIC
MEDICINE AND SURGERY

Ordinarily, the medical or surgical separation of a human organ from its power its based upon diseased, or otherwise defective, organs and tissues, and is corrective in character. Even heart transplants are intended to be corrective, and are done for the sake of the person's circulatory power. The separation of a defective heart is done in order to replace it with a healthy heart.

But the contraceptive separation of an organ from its power, by surgical, chemical or mechanical means, is not ordinarily based upon diseased, or upon otherwise defective organs and tissues, and is therefore not corrective in character. Where disease or other defects are involved, corrective measures may turn out to be indirectly contraceptive. But the directly contraceptive separation of an organ from its power, where no corrective purpose against disease or other defects in the organ is involved, is not comparable to corrective procedures in medicine and surgery, and has an entirely different meaning. A truthful comparison with a heart transplant would be something like a uterus transplant to correct a defective generative system. The meaning of this medical-surgical procedure, so similar to heart or kidney transplants, would be diametrically opposed to the meaning of contraception.

It is true that the surgeon cuts through good tissue in order to remove or repair defective tissue. But this cutting must not be judged on a peephole or physicalistic basis. For example, there is a great difference between cutting good tissue in order to kill a person, and doing the same in order to perform ther-

apeutic surgery. The act of cutting good tissue must be judged
for what it is in its entire context. Some will say that "contraceptive surgery" must be judged in this way too. But it cannot!
Therapeutic surgery is never a case of internally separating a
personally chosen act of communication from one of its fully
human powers. Because contraception is such a separation, it is
falsely compared to therapeutic medicine or surgery.

If an eye or another organ becomes cancerous, this part of
the person ought to be treated, or possibly removed, for the good
of the person. Similarly, if the sex organs or glands become
diseased, these ought to be treated, or possibly removed, for
the person's good. But contraception does not compare with
these cases, since it does not remove, or displace, a diseased or
otherwise defective part of the generative system.

What about instances when a healthy kidney is removed
from a living person for the sake of another person's life? Surgery
is performed, not to remove a diseased or defective organ, but
to remove a healthy organ. In such a case there is still no comparison with contraception. The healthy kidney is *given* so that
another person may have life; contraception is practiced so
that another person may not be given the gift of life. The removed kidney is transplanted to another person for corrective
purposes; contraception has no corrective purpose in the generative system. In the person from whom the healthy kidney
is removed, there is still another kidney to sustain the urological
power; contraception leaves the generative power unsustained.
Nor does the removal of the healthy kidney take place so that
a personally chosen action may be separated from one of the
powers internally structured in this action. Continence would be
more similar to the sacrifice of a healthy kidney; continence can
be a true sacrifice of oneself for the good of another person. Of
these forms of sacrifice it has been said that a man can have
no love greater than that by which he lays down his very life
for one he loves.

From these examples it may be clearly understood that biological correctness, or interference with biological correctness, is not the basis for defining the meaning of contraception, or for comparing other procedures with contraception. In coming to understand the meaning of contraception, biological correctness is beside the point. Biological correctness is not a moral issue in judging the removal of a healthy kidney that another person might have life; it is not a moral issue in judging contraception. Rather than biological correctness, the relation of an *interpersonal action with an interpersonal power internally present in this action* is the basis for understanding the meaning of contraception.

The popular view that medical reduction of infant deaths, and medically increased life expectancy, are interferences with nature, is a view that demands greater reflection. Rather, it is death and disease that are interferences with life and health. And it is these interferences with nature that medical science counteracts. Medicine and surgery for corrective purposes are attacks on interferences with personal nature, and are not themselves such interferences.

Medicine is helpful, not only for corrective, but also for preventive purposes. Inoculations to immunize against disease are acts of self-defense against interferences with health and life. Again, it is not life or health that is prevented, but death and disease.

When a chemical is used, not for correction or prevention of disease, but directly for contraceptive purposes, it becomes a medication that is used without a therapeutic purpose. Pills are taken to suppress disease germs or the germ producing processes that result in disease. But the germ cells of human life are not disease germs. It would be starkly Manichean to suppose that they are.

The process of ovulation is neither a disease nor a symptom of disease. But the ovum is, at least, a participating cause, though not the essential cause, of the problem that directly contraceptive chemicals are used to remedy. One might call over-population a disturbance of society, and ovulation some kind of causal agent in this disturbance. Yet, we all know that the ovum would not be such a causal agent without the sperm cell that activates it. Nor would the sperm and ovum unite without the interpersonal human action that is the original cause of human generation. If over-population is a social distress, the principal cause of this distress must be that which originally brings it into existence. Contraceptive measures, chemical as well as mechanical and surgical, are ways of trying to prevent a social disturbance without touching the initiating and principal cause of the disturbance. When those means are regarded as the solution to the problem, they only aggravate the real problem — a defective kind of conjugal love.

Today we have a situation in which millions of healthy women are taking potent drugs with many disturbing side-effects 20 days a month for long periods of time. Some of the effects caused by the drug are nausea, vomiting, cramps and bloating, amenorrhea, edema, chloasma (brownish discoloration of the skin), cerebral vascular accidents, vision impairment, loss of scalp hair, leg cramps, jaundice, migraine, allergic rash, rise in blood pressure, mental depression and blood clotting sometimes resulting in serious damage and strokes. It is true to say that the pill, instead of being a therapeutic medication, actually causes ailments and defects, as well as disease. Furthermore, detectable amounts of the active ingredients in oral contraceptives have been identified in the milk of mothers receiving these drugs. The effect of this dose on the infant drinking the milk has not been determined. Besides serious side-effects, there is a factor of death in connection with the pill that ought to cause apprehension. (Cf., *"The Pill"*; An Alarming Report, by Morton Mintz, Fawcett Publications, Greenwich, Conn., 1969.)

If one were to describe the condition of a woman taking the

oral contraceptive, even one who experiences no distressing side-effects, he would have to describe her condition as being abnormal. Menstruation without ovulation is a disorder in the generative system induced by the pill. Pregnancy symptoms without pregnancy is a disorder in the generative system induced by the pill. Instead of correcting disorders, the oral contraceptive creates disorders. It is a medication without a medically corrective purpose, and without a medically preventive purpose, in the sense of preventing disease rather than preventing the generation of life.

Even in cases where another pregnancy might result in serious illness or death for the mother, the oral contraceptive acts by preventing the pregnancy, a normal result, and not by preventing the defect or correcting the condition that makes a pregnancy dangerous. When, on the other hand, the pill is taken to bring about conception in a woman otherwise unable to conceive, it is taken for a medically corrective purpose even while acting temporarily as a contraceptive. In this case, the primary purpose for which the pill is taken is not contraception, but conception. Due to these careful, but essential distinctions, the definition of contraception might be extended as follows: an internal separation of the coital act from its generative power *for the direct purpose* of preventing conception, and without a medically therapeutic effect.

If some kind of contraceptive chemical is taken to regulate the menstrual cycle, the cycle definitely should be disordered and not just irregular. The cycle does not have to be mechanically regular in order to be normal. The human body is not a machine. A certain thought can make the heart beat faster. Psychic conditions can change the patterns in eating and digestion as well as in ovulation. It is normal for physical processes to be affected by psychic changes. If contraceptive chemicals are really therapeutic, there must be some hope of actually correcting a truly defective menstrual cycle so that the use of the chemicals may be terminated.

The control of population should be done by corrective or preventive means that are proportionate to the principal cause of human conception. Chemical, surgical or mechanical means of contraception are not proportionate to the principal cause of human conception. If medical science is to be adequate in this matter, it must provide an acceptable means for regulating coital activity, the personal and principal cause of conception. Either by providing a knowledge of the time of ovulation, or by prescribing a drug, in certain cases, to initiate ovulation so that its time will be known, the regulation of conceptional actions might be achieved. Also, pills taken to slow down a drive toward sexual activity, or sleeping pills, though undesirable alternatives, nevertheless would be proportionate to the principal cause of conception, and would be more accurate as corrective or modifying medical prescriptions than pills taken to separate the coital act from its generative power for the purpose of preventing conception.

Finally, any comparison of contraception with therapeutic medicine or surgery leads not only to a false rationale for justifying contraception, but also to a dangerous alignment of this type of comparison with medically induced or surgically performed abortions. An unwanted child readily may be, and often is, viewed as unwanted growth to be therapeutically removed. But on the basis of this same principle, many types of people: the crippled, incurable, aged and senile, criminals, mentally ill, mentally retarded and others may be viewed as a serious threat to the welfare of society, and as unwanted people to be therapeutically removed. Actually, there is no kind of human action, whether killing, lying, stealing, fornication, adultery or any injustice, that cannot be rationalized as being, in some way, a therapeutic measure.

Chapter 5

COMPARISONS WITH OTHER FORMS
OF SELF DEFENSE

When he is confronted by any agent, human or otherwise, that seriously threatens his life or health, the person spontaneously tends to defend himself. Corrective and preventive medicine and surgery are forms of self defense. War against an unjust aggressor may be done in self defense. Based upon the person's right to life, the act of killing an attacker in self defense can be justifiable, and would not be called murder.

Where there exists a real danger of being attacked by a rapist, a woman who uses some kind of contraceptive is acting in self defense. This defensive action cannot even be included within the definition of contraception as an internal separation of the coital act from its generative power, since the forceful coercion of a rapist is not a coital act — one with unitive or communicative value. For the purpose of self defense, a woman separates her generative organs from her generative power, but she does not separate a coital act from its generative power. As shown above, biological correctness is beside the point in assessing the meaning of contraception. The use of contraceptives is not necessarily an act of contraception.

Similarly, when the very life or basic welfare of a person or nation is seriously threatened, an act of deception in self defense is not necessarily an act of lying. The deception may be an external compliance with demands the attacker has no right to make. Lying can take place only on the basis of a condition of communication. Any use of force is not such a condition. In such a case, a deception cannot rightly be called a lie as a violation of human communication. Both lying and contraception must be defined on the basis of authentic conditions for human intercourse. Also, in a case of extreme hunger, the act of taking food that belongs to someone else is an act of self defense, and cannot rightly be called stealing. In such extreme situations — the use of contraceptives, the deception and the act of taking the goods of another — are as different from contraception, lying and stealing respectively as the act of killing another person in self defense is different from murder.

When a family is already large, and when the existing members are struggling to survive, the potential "invader" at the door of life may be viewed as a threat to the economic, social and psychic life of the family. It may seem that the family in its leaders, like a nation defending itself against invaders that threaten its total existence and economic-social stability, ought to defend itself by means of contraceptives. But, as in the other cases of extremity referred to above, this is not a case of direct defense against an unjust or hostile aggressor. The parents themselves are the ones who would bring the "invader" to the door of life; new persons do not come into a family by their own action, much less by aggressive or hostile intent. Actually, there is no one there to defend oneself against except one's own self. By internally separating his coital acts from his generative power, the person defends himself against himself. Contraceptives are used as armament against one's own being and defective acts of love. If the person thinks that he is *protecting* himself against his own biology, he implies that his biology, or his body, and his person are not really integrated. As such, his action is not defensive, but offensive. He declares a kind of aggressive war against his own person.

Chapter 6

AN AUTHENTIC COMPARISON

The similarity between the communication of coital intercourse and the communication of verbal dialogue seems to be a
strong basis for an elucidation of the meaning of contraception.

Both forms of human intercourse are voluntary or personally
chosen actions. Both result in conception. Coital intercourse is
fruitful in the conception of a child. Verbal intercourse is
fruitful in the conception of ideas and the development of
these ideas in the womb of the mind. The words expressed in
verbal dialogue are physical sounds produced by physical organs,
and are voluntarily spoken. Once the words are physically
uttered, the physical aspect of the movement of sound takes its
own course, just as the generative substance takes its own course
once it is voluntarily expressed in coital union.

Each form of communication is both communal and conceptional in nature. The experience of being-together, and conceptional fruitfulness, are correlative values in both verbal and
coital intercourse. In verbal dialogue, this communal aspect of
communication is expressed by the feeling tone of the voice,
attitudes of the person, gesticulation with the hands, certain
bodily movements and facial expression. And in coital intercourse, the communal relationship is expressed in a still more
extensive bodily articulation of presence and feeling. Despite
the striking differences that exist between mental and coital
intercourse, the similarity of these acts is substantial enough to
be revealing.

In both forms of communication, not all acts of intercourse
result in conception. One person may try to express an idea to
another repeatedly before the other understands. The generative

power of the mind is not always ready for activation. Similarly, not every act of coital expression is actually generative.

On the basis of these similarities between the mental and more properly sexual forms of human intercourse, contraception is like communicating words of love to one's spouse while preventing the sound waves of these words from reaching the other person. We can imagine that ear stopples or chemicals might be used to prevent the conception of ideas in the womb of the mind. In each of these ways, the act of communicating is internally separated from its mentally generative power.

Though the above examples seem farfetched and unrealistic, they do help to expose the meaning of separating an interpersonal action from a power internally structured in this action. More realistic examples of interference with mental communication, and ones more proportionate to the nature of mental life and expression, are lying, rationalization, refusal to receive the words of another in listening, or closing one's mind in the face of someone who is cherished as a loved person. All of these actions can be done without the use of devices, chemicals or surgery. But they are separations of a human action from one of its powers and are comparable with contraceptive separation.

Lying is an internal separation of a communicative act from its power to express and generate judgments truthfully. In his reflection upon his own judgments, the person judges them to be true, false or doubtful. If he tries to communicate as true a statement that he himself judges to be false, he separates his act of communication from his reflective judgment. This separation is not effected when he speaks in such a way to his dog, or to a wall, but only when the act of communication is fulfilled by being received through the listening and judging powers of another person. It is possible to communicate judgments by gestures, nods and other signs, as well as by speaking. But the meaning of the term "communicative act" in the definition of lying, when the act is one of speaking, is much more complex than simply uttering articulated sounds into the air. It is an interpersonal act that is not communicative unless accompanied by listening. As a communicative act, speaking is a sharing with another person who has a right to know what the speaker judges to be true, false or doubtful. When separation is offered under the guise of union, or falsity under the guise of truth, the lie comes into existence. Where there is no communal relationship, as in a case where the other person has no right to such a relationship, and where force is being used, the articulation of statements and other signs to express as true what is judged to be false does not fulfill the definition of a lie. Such speech is as different from interpersonal or communal speech as copulation under the force of a rapist who has no right to union is different from the coital act.

At times, there are truths that other persons should not know. Some truths should not be expressed. But these situations can be sustained without lying. When speech is internally separated from judgment, truth is not simply being withheld. It is made to become a guise for a statement that the speaker internally judges to be false.

In verbal communication, then, lying is an act which prevents the conception of truth right within the very act of presenting something as true. In coital communication, contraception is an act which prevents the conception of life right within the very act of presenting that which conceives life. These definitions and descriptions of lying and contraception reveal their basic similarity.

Rationalization is an internal form of lying in which the person prevents the conception of truth in his own mind. The chemical manipulation of germ-producing processes via the anovulant pill, and the mental manipulation of sources of judgment done by rationalizing, have much in common. Also, the closing of one's mind while pretending to listen is comparable to the use of a diaphragm while pretending to receive the conceptive substance of the husband.

Though contraception seems to be more physical in nature, and lying more mental in nature, both are separations of personally chosen communicative action from a power internally structured in this action.

Chapter 7

CONTRACEPTION AND ABORTION

When the practice of contraception is largely based upon the assumption that the human generative power is nothing more than a biological function, this assumption predisposes people for thinking that the result of the generative power, the embryo or fetus, is an effect no greater than its biological cause. As a result, many people, including scientists and philosophers, think that the embryo or fetus is nothing more than biological tissue, and not a human being at all. Abortion then becomes much more easily acceptable.

One of the basic principles of all human judgment is the principle of causality. Intuitively, we know that an effect cannot be greater than its cause. A new plant is a vegetative organism produced by the vegetative power of another plant, and is an effect no greater than its cause. A new animal is a biological organism with a sensient nature that is no greater than its reproductive source in other animals. If the human generative power is nothing more than a biological cause, how can the result of this power, the beginning of a new human being, be anything more than biological growth? Admittedly, this growing tissue would have to become more than merely biological somewhere along the line, otherwise the human person would never come into existence. But this change could take place only if another cause, a cause other than the generative power, steps in to produce a person. Traditionally, this other cause was thought to be God.

But we must begin to wonder why the human generative power is not fully adequate for being the cause of its effect — the new human person. If one part of the person has a biological origin, and if another part has a supernatural origin, as traditionally supposed, then the human being is difficult to understand as a fully integral *natural* unity. In the traditionalist perspective, God was posited as the cause of the person because it was rightly understood that the human spirit does not emerge from matter and that an effect cannot be greater than its cause.

Though it is true that the human person does not originate from biological matter as the sole cause of his being, this does not seem to be a sufficient reason for positing God as the cause that steps into a biological process to transform biological tissue into a person. There is no real reason why God should reserve for His own direct interference what He, as Creator, can give to the co-creative power of nature itself. This would mean that the human person, in and through his generative power, is endowed by God to be the fully adequate and sole immediate cause for the generation of other persons.

It is true that no person can create others as God creates being. There is no creation on the part of creatures, unless it is ultimately a co-creation together with the original Creator. In the most basic sense, God is the sole creator of each human being. But God is able to create the natural causes for the generation, in time, of new persons, and He is able to build all these natural causes into the co-creative power of nature itself. This would mean that the human generative power is much more than biological, and capable of co-creating much more than a biological effect. Man's generative power would then be understood as the sole *immediate* cause of its effect — the new human person.

But, though the human generative power might be regarded as the fully adequate cause of its effect, we might wonder when this effect emerges from its cause. Though conception may be viewed as a process, there is a moment in this process when the germ cells give way to a new type of cell; conception is completed *before* this first new cell divides to become an organism of two cells. But, is this single new cell the beginning of a new person? Many people would not think so. Some say that the zygote (the new cell following conception), the embryo or fetus are only a piece of tissue of the mother's body; others say these are stages of a living organism with no more value than an animal. Still others say that the growing entity in the uterus becomes a human being at one or other stage of development: implantation, fetal stage, quickening, viability or birth. Some even say that the human being comes into existence only when abstract reasoning begins.

But no one can rightly deny that a new life begins at the time of conception. Moreover, this new life is not a piece of tissue of the mother's body because it has an entirely different genetic dyamism than any living tissue of the mother's, or the father's, body. Furthermore, it is false to say that the intrauterine organism is of no more value than an animal, because no animal organism has ever been known to develop into a human being.

All doubts, possibilities and probabilities aside, most people would agree that the child is a human being at birth. But it seems unreasonable to think that the movement from one place to another, however dramatic, brings the person into existence. The reality of the human being does not depend upon location in this way. The spaceman suspended outside his capsule has as umbilical cord, but when he returns to the earth, he disposes of this cord. The presence or absence of an umbilical connection has nothing to do with his status as a human being. Similarly, if the child is human outside the uterus, he is human before he leaves it.

But sometimes it is argued that the child, though he is physically formed like a human being at birth, is not a person until he manifests the psychic characteristics of human life. In other words, the reality of the person is thought to exist in psychic rather than in physical life. Since it is the quality of psychic life that distinguishes the human person from other

living ,things, it is possible to insist that the person comes into
existence only when he becomes aware of himself at about the
age of two years. Still, the child at this age is just passing out
of the stage of the psychic embryo. Does he become a person,
then, only when he is able to begin abstract thinking around the
ages of five or six? After all, it is easy enough to believe that
the ability for abstract thinking is the line of demarcation between human and subhuman beings. It might be argued, then,
that the birth of reason is the birth of the person.

But we can readily see, that of all these possibilities, one is
really as good as the other. Furthermore, human beings often
remain little more than embryonic in their intellectual and
spiritual development. Scientists say that only a small percentage
of the brain potential of the adult is ever realized. A case could
be made for saying that many human adults do not become
human persons.

But potentiality is a kind of actuality. The capacity for
reasoning is an existing potential in the human kind of awareness that is self-awareness. What appears at ages five or six, the
evidence of abstract reasoning, existed potentially, and even
implicitly, in the self-awareness at age two. This self-awareness
may be, already, a minimal kind of reasoning. Though the child
is not actually reasoning in an explicit manner, his power for
reasoning is an actuality. Furthermore, the self-awareness at
age two was actually present, as a capacity, in the child's brain
at birth. And his particular kind of brain really existed as a
capacity in the zygote at the time of conception. Though the
zygote did not have a brain, the very dynamism of the human
brain existed at conception.

Being must be distinguished from *having*. The *being* of the
human brain is *actually* present in the zygote, though the child
in that stage of life does not *have* a brain. The animal zygote
does not develop a human brain because the being of the
human brain is not present in the animal zygote. Thus, the

human zygote is qualitatively different (different in the kind of being that is) from the animal zygote. The capacity for reasoning actually exists at conception, and may even be implicitly operative, though it becomes explicitly operative only several years after birth. No such capacity actually exists in the animal zygote; or if it did, why does it not become manifest? In other words, why don't animals become humans?

Those who deny that the human person exists at conception often think in terms of a functional definition of person. Thus, they are inclined to think that the person exists only when he actually functions as one. But the human zygote has all the capacities for functioning as a person, and these capacities indicate the real presence of a person. The human zygote, embryo or fetus does not have to look like a person, or act like a person, in order to BE a person. It is scientifically naive to judge by immediate appearances. Judging in this way, people falsely believed for centuries that the sun moved around the earth. Though some people with a functional definition of person may seem to argue convincingly that the human *person* does not exist at the time of conception, they cannot argue convincingly that the human *being* does not exist at the time of conception. And a human being is always a human person. As a zygote or embryo, the person does not seem to have a personality. But though the person is the basis of personality, their meanings are not the same.

From the viewpoint of the biologist, an acorn is just an acorn with the potential to become an oak tree. The biologist does not concern himself with the fact that the fertilized seed actually IS an oak tree. The dynamic *being* of an oak tree is present in the acorn, though the trunk, roots, branches and leaves are not yet expressed. Even when the tree is fully developed, these parts are expressions, or internal revelations, of its original being that was actually present as a result of fertilization.

Those who call the human embryo or fetus a potential person

that is not really a person are unaware of the dynamic reality of being. The human zygote could not even have the potencies it has unless its very being warranted such capacities.

If we do not hold that *all* the capacities of the human being are actually present in the zygote, we will be forced to hold that the human being is some kind of artifact. Artifacts are made by forming parts and then putting these parts together from without. This is man's way of making *things*. But it is not the way of natural genesis in which the whole being comes into existence from within. In the making of artifacts, parts of a thing are formed before that thing — a table, clock, painting, book or house, is completed. To think that conception is followed by mere tissue growth needed to support the reality of a person is to project falsely man's way of forming artifacts into the much more total genesis of natural beings.

Those who think that the human zygote, containing the full genetic dynamism for the adult person, is like the blueprint for a house, forget that the blueprint is external to the house, and that the house is only an artifact of man. The "blueprint" of a person, however, is always internal to his being, and is not the "blueprint" of his *being* but of the parts of his being. The person is not an artifact, but is a natural being developing his own parts from within himself. Thus, it is false to say that the human zygote *is* a genetic blueprint; it *is* a human being that *has* a genetic structure.

And those who think that the body must attain a human shape before the soul is infused to take over the body do not realize how similar this is to making a motor, pouring gasoline into it, and then starting the motor. Organisms begin with all their parts existing together in an implicit manner; growth is the process of differentiating the fully given; it is the internal revelation of the *being* that is present in its own beginning at the time of conception.

If the human embryo has a plant soul at first, as some

philosophers seem to think, this plant soul animates something that is being formed into an animal body. When the animal body is formed in and through the plant soul, then the animal soul takes over. A human body is then formed in and through this animal soul. Finally, when the human body is formed, the human soul animates this body. But how can a plant soul animate something that is forming an animal body? If an animal body is being formed, an animal soul is being revealed in this process, just as the formation of a plant body reveals the dynamic being of a plant. And how can an animal soul animate something that is forming a human body? If a human body is being formed, the dynamic being of a human person is revealed in this process.

If, on the other hand, the human shape is supposed to exist before the human being can exist, then the shape of a plant in roots, stem, branches and leaves would have to exist before the life principle of the plant could enter this shape. What kind of soul or life principle then animates the thing that is growing into a plant? It would have to be a pre-vegetative or mineral soul. But this is utterly unacceptable. From all the evidence of nature, a *plant soul* exists only in something that is forming a *plant body*, and an *animal soul* exists only in something that is forming an *animal body*. Otherwise, the matter and the life principle of an organism would be conceived as being artificially put together and far from dynamically integrated.

Furthermore, when the human embryo is moving from the so-called plant stage to the so-called animal stage, there is no discoverable difference in the type of cell that composes the organism. The cell does not change from a plant to an animal type. And, in the movement from the so-called animal stage to the human, there is, again, no discovered difference in the type of cell in the growing being. From the time of conception, the quality of each cell is human, and is described as having the 46 chromosomes that will be present in every cell of the adult human being. It is unthinkable that a human-type cell cluster is the natural and spontaneous expression of a plant soul. If the human embryo had a plant soul, it would have a plant type of cell within it.

The best part of the human mind is painfully jarred when forced to think that a woman conceives a plant type of entity in her womb, and that this organism becomes an animal before it becomes a human being. This is an unperceptive view of ontogenesis. Ontogeny (individual development) recapitulates phylogeny (evolution of species) not literally, but only by vestige and similitude. In the words of the evolutionist, Teilhard de Chardin, the beginning of a new kind of being in the evolution of species is a "leap from zero to everything," and not a gradual process at all. No less is true of the beginning of each being within a species. Conception is a leap from zero into a whole new being that manifests its original nature by its growth and development.

Some philosophers and theologians consider the phenomenon of identical twins to be grounds for arguing against the existence of the human being at conception. They rightly insist that the zygote which divides in half cannot be interpreted as one human being dividing into two. But this impossibility still does not rule out the existence of the human person at conception. When the zygote divides, resulting in identical twins, this effect cannot be greater than its cause. The cause is both internal and environmental (intrauterine). It may be considered internal to the original cell-cluster on hereditary or chromosomal grounds, meaning that another being is possible in the one cell-cluster from the time of conception. This second being would become actual only if environmental conditions trigger the twinning process. In that case, the result would be something similar to what scientists are now saying about the possibility of inducing embryogenesis in a cell of the adult person's body, and developing an identical twin for that person. Who, then, would be the parent of the new person? The adult would be the only parent of his twin. In a somewhat similar manner, the original zygote (a human being) becomes a parent of another in twinning, though it is much more difficult, and so far impossible in this instance, to tell which one is the parent.

However, there are some who think that if a cell of the human body other than the germ cells could be induced to develop into another human being, this would be evidence that the single cell produced by conception is no different from any other cell of the human body. And since other cells of the human body are not human persons, it is thought that the impregnated ovum is not a human person. But the fact remains that no other cell of the human body besides the impregnated ovum develops into another human being in ordinary circumstances. In the case of human genesis from a cell other than an impregnated ovum, if that were possible, the being of a new person would come into existence with the authentic *initiation* of embryogenesis.

Instances of a developing zygote becoming a mole on the wall of the uterus have been regarded as evidence that the zygote and embryo are developing tissue rather than a developing person. But there are many instances of faulty formation in the embryo and resultant birth defects or prenatal death. Degeneration of the person's developing body into a mole is one of the many tragic ways in which human beings are subject to deformity and death.

If the *being* of the person does not come into existence before the first division of the original cell that results from conception, the person is some kind of artifact made in a part-by-part manner. And all talk about the internal unity of the whole person, so important in the new personalist philosophy and theology, is unfounded wish-fulfillment.

The difference between the adult and the newborn is a matter of many years. But the difference between the newborn and the newly conceived is only a matter of months. If we hold that the adult and the newborn are human beings, how much more so are the newborn and the newly conceived of the same human nature?

The baby is a psychic zygote in the womb, and a psychic embryo after birth. This embryonic psychic life differentiates into the great complexity of emotions, attitudes, habits and mental processes of the adult. But there is no fundamental change in psychic life from the time of conception to adulthood. As there is a *human* continuity in psychic development, there is a *human* continuity in physical development from conception to maturity.

Behind the various ways of questioning and doubting that the human zygote, embryo or fetus is a human person is the very real implication of the assumption that the human generative power is nothing more than a biological function. When the human generative power is regarded as simply biological, the fruit of this power, by inexorable laws of logic, must be viewed as being nothing more than biological growth. Thus, the assumption behind the arguments for contraception becomes the assumption for allowing and, in many cases, actually accepting abortion.

Besides the willingness of many people to permit the surgical slaughter of the uterine person, there are others who have no reservations about using the IUD, a birth preventive device that is strongly suspected to be abortifacient. At the present time, two kinds of abortion drugs are nearing or may already have reached the market: the "morning-after" pill and the Swedish "M-pill." Many women who now use contraceptives more than likely will change to these abortifacients when they are available. This will happen particularly if the abortifacients are more convenient, more effective, having less unwanted side effects, and if they are cheaper than contraceptive pills. Already, a very high percentage of the so-called contraceptive pills now in use, particularly the low dosage pills are suspected to be abortifacients; some are even advertized as such in medical journals.

Thus, a widespread acceptance of contraception predisposes people for abortion, especially those who are unreflective and who think that matters of sex are not things to be thought about as much as things just to be done. Where people are unreflective, there is a falling-domino relationship between contraception and abortion. The strong movement toward legalized abortion in our own country was preceded by legalized contraception.

But this gradual degeneration conflicts with the basic principles of our democracy, particularly with the equal right of all to life. If human beings have no right to life from the time of conception, is there any other right they can really have? In our society, a man is judged to be innocent until proven guilty. It should be held also that the human zygote or embryo is a human being with human rights until proven otherwise. And who can prove that a human being does not exist at the beginning of *his own growth?*

Most people condemn the deathcamps of Nazi Germany. But the attitude toward human life that perpetrated these horrors still lives in the world. From the viewpoint of the Nazi scientists, the Jews and other unwanted persons were not really human, but just part of nature. Unwanted persons were defined outside the class of humanity precisely because they were regarded as unwanted. More and more, the uterine person is being evaluated in the same way. How else account for the 25-30 million abortions estimated to have taken place in the world during the year 1968, with this monstrous number rapidly increasing since then?

The increasing use of killer-chemicals for birth prevention, besides the increase of surgical abortions throughout the world, makes the uterine deathcamp a stark and horrible fact. Yet, the cries of protest are no louder today than they were when the

Nazis exterminated the unwanted Jews. Six million Jews will be minimal in comparison to the numbers that already are, and that continue to be, exterminated by abortion. Will history eventually show, after our conscience becomes sensitized on this matter, that the greatest killers have not been men with their wars, but women with their own indwelling children? The action that is demanded must be vitalized and encouraged by a profound re-thinking of the whole issue of man-woman relationships and their power to generate new human life.

Chapter 8

THE ART OF REGULATING CONCEPTION

The regulation of conception may be not only a good, but also a necessity, for any given family. Just as the principal cause of conception, the coital act, is meant to be treated as a human art, conception regulation should be treated as a fully human *art*, and not just a matter of scientific technology. Conception regulation is primarily the regulation of the whole person in his coital activity, an *art* that incorporates scientific technology without a utilitarian abandonment to it. Since the power to generate new life is a power of the whole person, the regulation of this power should be a matter of self-regulation and not merely a control of biology.

Just as there are times when truth should not be spoken, there are times when children should not be conceived. But the act of refraining from speaking differs essentially from the act of internally separating speech from its power truthfully to express and generate judgments in the mind of another. Similarly, the act of refraining from coital activity differs essentially from the act of internally separating coital union from its generative power.

By their very nature, some coital acts do not engage their generative power. These acts simply do not have the natural result of generation, though they are still internally united with their generative power. Internal union of act and power does not imply a necessary activation of the generative power by the coital act. Because he has the freedom to choose whether or not he will engage in coital activity at all, the human person is free to choose between generative and non-generative coital acts. And his freedom to choose whether or not he will engage in coital activity is much greater than his freedom to choose whether or not he will eat food; the latter choice is more deeply conditioned by organismic necessity than the former.

As the generation of new persons is a marital action shared by two persons contemporaneously, the regulation of conceptions should be a marital act shared by two persons at once. Conception regulation by periodic continence is impossible without both persons sharing the choice and responsibility at once. For this reason, it is proportionate to the marriage relationship itself. With contraception, on the other hand, one person at a time can easily use means for preventing conception.

Besides engaging both persons together, the art of periodic continence involves the total person of each. It includes psychic, mental and spiritual action as well as physiological consideration. While contraception is an investment of birth control in devices and chemicals, periodic continence is an investment in the whole person. Devices such as the calendar and thermometer are used as helps for integrating the process of ovulation into personal knowledge and understanding. Conception regulation, if it is to be proportionate to the person and to the marriage relationship between two persons, should be as psychological and as spiritual as it is physical. And it should be as psychic, spiritual, physical and interpersonal *in its method* as marital love itself.

When conception control is wholly invested in devices and chemicals, and no effort made to assimilate the generative power into personal knowledge and understanding, these items become substitutes for a fully human art. The effort to follow, through scientific means, the rhythms of fertility can hardly be compared to the simple, direct and efficient suppression of this rhythm by the anovulant pill, or to the internal separation of this rhythm from the coital act by other contraceptives. Conception regulation by periodic continence respects the real distinction between the coital act and its generative power, but contraception reduces the distinction to a separation.

When people think that human generation is solely a biological event rather than a totally human event, it is then logical to think that a control of the generative power ought to be a control of biology alone. However, contraception does not control, but suppresses, biology. There is a great difference between control and suppression. For instance, controlling the activities of a two-year-old child is essentially different from suppressing his activities by staking his feet to the ground. Similarly, controlling the human generative power by knowledge of ovulation and by periodic continence is essentially different than forcefully putting the generative power out of action and out of attention with contraceptives.

When the generative power is put out of action, and out of attention, in the very act that would render this power active, it is radically separated from its human context. The person tries to reduce this power to the level of mere biology. By separating the generative power from its totally human context, contraception is an attempt to biologize, and thus to depersonalize, this power. Consequently, the separation is a dehumanization and a devaluation of the personal nature of the human generative power. With contraception, the person intends to render a potentially generative interpersonal action non-generative; with periodic continence, what would be a potentially generative interpersonal action is not engaged.

But it has been argued that periodic continence, while it respects the physiological rhythm of persons, interferes with their psychic rhythm. It is claimed that the coital expression of love must be turned on and off artificially, and that the spontaneity of emotion is violated. Many say that though the coital act and its generative power are not separated by periodic continence, the very persons who are two in one flesh are separated.

Periodic continence is declared to be just as artificial as contraception.

But if this is the case, would it not likewise be that a mother who is faced with the tremendous challenge of controlling the behavior of her two-year-old runabout may readily say that this demand for control interferes with her psychic desires and tendencies. If she abandons the challenge and ties the child to a tree or stakes his feet to the ground, she will be more free to follow spontaneously her own psychic life. It is clear that in this latter case she is imposing an exceedingly artificial existence on the child, but it is not so clear that in the first case she is really imposing an artificial existence on herself. Human effort and control are not necessarily artificial. It is only the lack of a creative attitude toward this effort and control that renders it, in some sense, artificial. The control of an active child is a great art, and one that requires love, respect, affirmation and knowledge on the mother's part. But suppressing rather than regulating the child's activity is no art at all.

Conception regulation by period continence is rarely viewed as a human art. It has been criticized as being similar to shaking hands with a friend only if he comes at a certain time of the month. But sustaining this example, contraception is like going to put on gloves or using some kind of chemical or mechanical protection before shaking hands with a friend so that contamination by his germs may be prevented. Is shaking hands really that important? The free person knows that there are other ways of warmly greeting a friend.

Insofar as he loves himself and another, the human person is free *to* express himself or *not to* express himself in any given way. If he were not free not to express a certain idea that comes to his mind, his expression would be necessitated. Unless the person is free *not to* express a thought or feeling, he is not free *to* express that thought or feeling.

Just as he is able to express thought in many ways, the

human person is capable of expressing love in many ways. If coital intercourse is the only spontaneous way of communicating marital love, then the love, freedom, spontaneity and sexuality of the persons are grossly undifferentiated. But such a differentiation of the person is necessary for maturation. If periodic continence can help to differentiate persons so that love may be spontaneously expressed in more than one way, and so that the coital act may be spontaneously expressed only on the basis of respect for its generative power, then periodic continence is highly desirable for the sexual maturation of married people. As this maturation progresses, continence becomes less and less difficult, and more integrated into the art of marital life.

Such a development is required of any art. At first, the art of piano playing requires practice, exercise and work without much spontaneity. Only after the art is somewhat developed does spontaneity appear. But this developed spontaneity is much more refined and differentiated than that of the child who spontaneously pounds the piano before the discipline of lessons and practice begins. Similarly, coital activity may have an undeveloped spontaneity at first. But as it becomes modified through the art of conception regulation, this spontaneity may diminish for a time only to emerge again in a more highly developed form.

While the persons progress through the first stages in developing the art of self-regulation, the periods without coital activity may seem to be periods of continence or abstinence, or a kind of discipline similar to the discipline required in learning any art. But once the spontaneity of the art begins to emerge, periods without coital activity are no longer experienced as being negative, but rather as another kind of positive fulfillment. The use of the terms continence and abstinence actually belongs more properly to periods without food and drink, than to periods without coital activity. The need for food and drink is based upon organismic necessity. But the coital expression of love is not meant to be based on organismic necessity. For this reason, the use of the terms continence and abstinence in sexuality is almost inevitably misleading.

Since conception regulation is also coital regulation, it implies a control not only of the generative power, but also of coital activity in which the generative power internally exists. As the pianist, in performing a great work of musical art, follows the rhythm of the written score, and does not abandon it for the sake of a more emotional rhythm of his own, married persons, in performing the art of coital love-expression, may follow the rhythm of their generative power written into their lives, and not abandon it for the sake of another more emotional rhythm.

Implicit in the choice of periodic continence over contraception is a respect for the total being of the persons involved. This respect can become an essential motivator in developing the art of regulating conception. Respect for the unity of the person, as well as for the interpersonal unity of the generative power, can become the mental, emotional and spiritual leaven that married people need in order to sustain the effort and practice required by their art.

Just as any art that is good in itself can be used for negative or selfish reasons, periodic continence, an art that is good in itself, can be used for selfish reasons. Contraception, neither an art nor a good it itself, can be used for a good *purpose*, that is, to limit the size of a family where this limitation is necessary. Contraception can be used also for selfish reasons. But the positive or negative purpose for which any one of these methods is used does not make the method itself positive or negative. It is not the purpose that makes the methods different; and no purpose can ever make them the same. They are essentially different as means to an end. No selfish purpose can make periodic continence a negation in itself, and no good purpose can make contraception a good in itself.

But when a negation is used for a creative purpose, as when a child's activity is suppressed to prevent him from receiving injury in an accident, the quality of the creative purpose is affected by the negation. And the quality of a good action done for a negative purpose is affected by that purpose. A woman who creatively regulates the activities of her child for a purpose other than the good of the child himself, changes the quality of her good action. Thus any art that is good in itself, but performed for selfish reasons, becomes affected, or modified, by its purpose.

If freedom, love and sexuality are differentiated so that married people have various ways of expressing themselves to each other, conception regulation can become an art as physically, psychically and spiritually total as coital love itself. But this process of differentiation always depends for its impetus and strength upon the way in which the persons think about their human nature and sexuality. Do they have an authentic philosophy and theology of their human being and their sexuality to act as an emotional-mental leaven in their life together? Without creative *meaning*, it is difficult to live a creative life. The widespread use of contraception is symptomatic of a lack of meaning in marriage. Marital communion does not live by needs and impulses alone, but also, and most importantly, by the meanings and values of *being*. There is a great need, today, for a revolutionary metaphysics of human being and sexuality. (Cf., *NEW DYNAMICS IN SEXUAL LOVE;* A Revolutionary Approach To Marriage and Celibacy, by Robert and Mary R. Joyce, St. John's University Press, Collegeville, Minnesota, 1970.)

Chapter 9

THE NATURE OF THE HUMAN PERSON

If dropped from a cliff, a man would fall like a rock. But this would not mean that he is a rock. Like plants, people grow and multiply. But they are not plants. And like animals they see and hear. But people are not animals. With his rock-like, plant-like and animal-like functions, the human person is in no sense a rock or a plant. And, most importantly of all, *he is in no sense an animal.*

Why, then, has man been defined as a rational animal? This definition implies that man is basically an animal, and that he differs from other animals simply by being rational. But there is nothing in man that is an animal structure or process, not even his digestion of food or elimination of wastes. These are animal-like processes, but not animal processes.

The human body in all its parts and in all its cells, including ova and sperm cells, is a revelation of the person's being within his being. The whole being of the person is present in each part of his body. Not even his liver or pancreas is the organ of an animal; it is the organ of a person. If the liver or pancreas of an animal were successfully transplanted in the body of a person, this organ would not function by the power of an animal's being, but by the power of a person's being. It would become a person-al organ. The definition of man as a rational animal is therefore a biological, and not a metaphysical, definition. Its frame of reference is the organism rather than the person. But man, if he is to be defined at all, must be defined on the basis of his personhood, and not on the basis of his animal-like functions.

Because we think of man as evolving from the animal kingdom, it is difficult not to think of him as coming from an animal of some kind. But man came from nature as a whole. Just as it is not really accurate to think of the hand as coming from the arm, though the hand comes from the person in and through his arm, it is not really accurate to think of man as coming from an animal of some kind, though he comes from nature as a whole, in and through the animal kingdom.

Evolution is the unfolding of the original energies of the created universe. And the natural energy of being that is revealed in human intelligence and love does not emerge *out of* the organic energy that is expressed in animal life. Rather, the basic energy of human existence emerges out of nature's co-creational depth and *assimilates into itself* the organic energy that is expressed in animal life. When man was about to appear in the world, the specifically human energy of nature assimilated into itself and completely transformed the organic energy of some animal species. This assimilation and transformation was so complete that the organic energy in man's being was no longer an animal energy, but a person-al energy. Thus, there never was a time when the being of man was that of an animal.

This process of assimilation and transformation is beautifully evident in the maturation of the human infant toward the activity of walking. Many animals are able to walk or run almost immediately after birth. Though he is born with a similar walking reflex, a vestige of evolution, the human infant is unable to walk. So the walking reflex disappears. And the baby lies on his back or stomach for months. Before he is able to walk, he must mentally absorb or *assimilate* his environment as the eventual context of his locomotion. And he must assimilate his legs and feet into his specifically human awareness. Only after the child has discovered his legs and feet as well as his environment is he ready to begin his arduous development of the art of walking. Unlike the walking of a lamb or foal, the walking of a baby is a human act with a foundation in human awareness and intelligence. At no time before or after birth is the human being an animal in any sense.

Because definition moves from the general to the specific, or from the common to the different, man's animal-like functions seem to base the definition of his nature in animality. But it would be better not to define man at all than to define his nature in this way. One of the unhappy results of such a definition has been the inadequate interpretation of human sexuality. Because it appears that man has sex in common with animals, his sexuality has been thought to exist primarily for the same purpose that sex exists in animals, that is, for reproduction. When man is thought to be basically an animal, it is logically consistent to hold that his sexuality, insofar as it is animal-like, exists basically for reproduction, and insofar as it is different from animal sexuality, exists only secondarily for that difference. But this way of thinking about man and his sexuality is no longer acceptable; it is biological rather than person-al.

Furthermore, rationality is not the most basic difference of man from animals. Intellectuality is the basis of rationality. The human intellect is largely intuitive and secondarily rational. Reasoning is a way of working out and strengthening intuitions. The intuitive dynamism of the intellect permeates, assimilates and transforms the person's sensations before these sensations terminate in his brain. As a result, hearing can become listening, and seeing can become observing. This largely pre-rational power of the human mind radically distinguishes man from animals. Thus, rationality, as the qualifying part of the definition "rational animal" is as misleading in coming to an understanding of human nature as is the basis of the definition in animality.

In the traditional view of human nature, a view within a biological frame of reference, the individual man is seen as a being enclosed within the boundaries of his skin; it is thought that his soul is contained within the physical boundaries of his body. Consequently, it is declared that nothing enters the mind except through the senses. The intellect must then wait upon the senses, as a passive receiver, for their physiological stimulation of the brain.

But the most vital dimension of human reality is not enclosed within physical limits, and the power of intellection is not enclosed within the limits of the senses. It is more true to the reality of the human person to think of his body as existing within his soul than to think of the soul as existing solely within the body. As the earth, in its mass and motion, exists within and expresses the gravitational and powerful energy-field surrounding and permeating it, the human body exists within and expresses the human spirit. The mass of the earth IS the cosmic energy-field as expressed in physical dimensions. Similarly, the human body IS the human spirit as expressed in physical dimensions. The senses and other organs of the body are then understood as expressions of the being of man *within* the depths of his being.

In the light of this metaphysical or truly personalist view of human reality, it is seen that the fundamental expanse of the person's being opens into the world beyond the physical boundaries of his body, and even beyond the scope of his bodily and psychic needs. Physiological needs for such things as food and oxygen show that man's being opens into the world and is not self-contained. Emotional needs for acceptance and security, as well as mental needs for knowledge, motivation and positive attitudes also reveal the person as a being extending beyond his physical boundaries into the universe. Still, this psychic life is not the most basic dimension of man's reality. His ability to be aware of his own awareness manifests a dimension of his being that is other than, though present within, his physical and psychic responses. We may call this other dimension *spiritual,* though the act of being aware of one's own awareness is as concrete as eating. This spiritual dimension, the source of reflexive awareness and other forms of intuitive knowing, is the most expansive and most open field of man's being, extending deeper and farther into the being of the world than his physical and psychic life.

But these three fields of man's being must not be conceived as separate or even separable things. All of them emanate from a single center of being, and are differentiations in the radical unity of one being. Within the dynamics of this unity, one field of the person's reality reveals the other and is assimilated within that other. But this revelation and assimilation *begins* not in the most obvious dimension of man's being, but in the basic, the spiritual dimension. Though the anatomical and physiological aspects of the person are the most apparent and the most immediate in his total needs they are not the most basic. Bodily needs for food and oxygen are assimilated into psychic needs for love, acceptance and security. Every psychologist knows, for instance, how deeply the simple function of eating is assimilated into the emotional life of the infant. But still more fundamentally, the emotional-mental life of the person is assimilated, even if only subconsciously, into his intuitive presence to the world and his reflexive awareness of himself and his environment.

Because of the spiritual field of his reality, the person's power to know the being of the world is in touch with the world before the physiological process of sensation terminates in the brain. The power of intuitive intellection assimilates and transforms this physiological process from within, so that it is never, at any moment, a simply biological process. The person's power to know being is in touch with the existence of things beyond-sensation-within-sensation. He knows their being pre-consciously before his senses actually bring him to a conscious knowledge of these things. Preconscious knowing, like the largest part of an island below the surface, precedes conscious knowing. When the being of the human person is understood as a physical field assimilated within and transformed by a psychic field, which is, in turn, assimilated within and transformed by a spiritual field, then it is understood that human knowledge is not limited to a biological frame of reference, but is basically trans-sensory and intellectually intuitive.

Underlying this way of thinking about man's nature is the reinterpretation of the human body as the internal expression of the human spirit. When we understand that the human body IS the human spirit, as expressed in a physical way, we also understand that the human body, while being physical, is much more than physical; it is primarily metaphysical. This distinction between the physical and the metaphysical aspects of the human body seems to support St. Paul's distinction between the "natural body," and the "spiritual body" (I Cor. 15:44). Or, as the same idea is expressed in another translation — "If the soul has its own embodiment, so does the spirit have its own embodiment. The first man, Adam, as scripture says, became a living soul; but the last Adam has become a life-giving spirit" (Jerusalem Bible).

This very meaningful distinction between soul and spirit is used by St. Paul to explain the spiritual body of the resurrected person. But it does not mean that the person has a soul and a spirit, or that he has two bodies. Instead, these distinctions point to various aspects of one and the same radically unified being. The human life principle, or spirit, may be seen from different points of view. From the viewpoint of the physical dimension of the body, this life principle may be called the soul. From the viewpoint of the metaphysical dimension of the body, the same life principle may be distinguished as the spirit. And it is true that these distinctions do help toward understanding what is meant by the resurrection of the body.

In fact, there is a kind of resurrection of the body already in this life. All the human processes of assimilation are kinds of resurrection. For example, the assimilation of the physical organs for walking into the mental life of the child is a kind of resurrection process — a drawing of legs and feet into a deeper life. The metaphysical dimension of the human body, or the spiritual body, is the crucial principle in this human process of assimilation. And this dynamic principle is so real in the here-and-now person, that it is the basis of his personal survival of death.

It is obvious that the person loses the physical dimension of his body in death. But the metaphysical dimension of his body remains internally united with his spirit, so that it is not only his spirit, but his entire person, that survives death. This is quite a different conclusion than that of the traditional view of human reality in which the soul is thought to survive death, but not the person. Since the person is seen as a unity of body and soul, and since death is seen as a separation of body and soul, death is thought to be the destruction of the person, though not the destruction of his soul. But, if the body and spirit of the human person can be separated, the *unity* of the person must be called into question. Much recent scientific evidence points to an absolute or complete unity of the person so that many who are influenced by this evidence think that the death of the human body must be a total destruction of the person. But, in this contemporary view, as well as in the traditional philosophy of human nature, the physical matter of the human body is thought to be the entire reality of this body. Neither of these views is based upon a metaphysical insight into the nature of human flesh.

Even in ordinary everyday life, the physical matter of the human body is not as stable as the body itself. Though changing in weight, shape and size, the same body remains. Most significantly of all, however, there is a complete turnover in the physical matter of the body every seven years. Yet the person's body remains stable through it all. Death seems to be this same process concentrated into a moment. What previously happened in seven years becomes sudden and complete. The physical matter of the body is completely expelled from the being of the person, though the unity of the person in his spirit and in the metaphysical dimension of his body survives death. The final resurrection would then be a re-expression of man's being in physical dimensions.

As a spoken word expresses the unity of the mind and its concept (a mental word), the physical space-time dimension of the human body expresses the unity of the human spirit and its spiritual body. Like the word that is spoken no longer, the physical expression of the flesh falls away in death, and the person becomes silent to this space-time dimension of the world. His presence is expressed in this way no longer. But a silent person may still be living, active and thinking, though he is neither heard nor seen.

This exquisitely profound unity of the person's being that survives even the radical trauma of death is certainly meant to survive the most challenging of moral situations in space-time life. The human person is called to *live* the unity of his being in abiding affirmation; each failure is a kind of moral death. Anyone who truly loves himself will receive as deeply as possible the unity of his being into his everyday life, and will accept this unity of being as the most basic law of the good life. In so doing, he gradually transcends the grasp of death that would hold him not only physically, but also morally and spiritually.

Chapter 10

THE SEXUALITY OF THE HUMAN PERSON

Just as the *totality* of human nature has been traditionally interpreted and defined in a biological frame of reference, every *particular aspect* of human nature, including knowledge and sexuality, has been interpreted and defined within a biological frame of reference. But, when it is seen within a beingful or metaphysical frame of reference that the human person is not enclosed within the boundaries of his skin, and that the power of intellection is not enclosed within the limits of the senses, it may also become clear that human sexuality is not enclosed within the limits of the sex organs. Based on the nature of the human person, the physical dimension of sexuality expresses the psychic dimension of sexuality. And the psychic expresses the spiritual. This means that human sexual energy is primarily spiritual in nature, secondarily psychic, and finally biological. Though human sexual energy is a unified totality, it is differentiated in the same way that human nature is differentiated.

Sexual differences in the bodies of men and women are not just biological differences; they are revelations of sexual differences in the depths of human reality. Due to a desire for establishing the equality of men and women, it is currently being thought by many that sexual differences are biological only, and that any differences other than the biological are due to cultural conditioning. If this were true, sex would be nothing more than an accidental, or a mere attachment to a human nature that is the same for both men and women. But the sexual dynamism permeates the human mind and feelings too deeply to be nothing more than an anatomical modification.

As the baby is not ready for walking when the walking

reflex appears, the adolescent is not ready for coital activity when the physiological impulses of sexuality first appear. Before the coital act can be a fully humanized act, the physiological dimension of sexual energy must be *assimilated* and *transformed* by the emotional, mental and spiritual dynamics of human sexual energy. It is not enough for a human person to have impulses and feelings; his most personal need is to be able to interpret and evaluate his impulses and feelings. When he is unable to do so, he either represses his impulses and feelings or allows them to have an unhumanized expression. This is particularly true in the area of sexuality.

The humanization process by which the physiological impulses of human sexual energy are assimilated into the mental and spiritual dynamics of sex may be called sublimation. But this meaning for the term is radically different from any other meaning. It is particularly different from the Freudian meaning for sublimation, a meaning within a biological frame of reference. According to Freud, the energy of sex is nothing more than a physiological energy that is sublimated by being redirected from physiological to social goals. He sees sublimation as a defense against repression, or as an unconscious way of reacting to social pressures. But when the nature of the human person is viewed from an entirely different perspective, sublimation is seen as a spontaneous process of human personalization. Even the mental preparation of the baby for walking, the assimilation of his legs, feet and environment into human awareness, and the act of walking itself are seen as examples of sublimation. And the evolution of sexuality in the person's life is a process of assimilation that is natural and necessary for growth. In its best meaning, then, sublimation is a process of human actualization; it is possible neither to animals nor to angels. In its most human meaning, it is neither a redirecting of an animal energy nor an angelization of man, but a most natural and spontaneous process of human growth. (For a more detailed description of sublimation, see my chapter on "Sexual Freedom Through Sublimation." reprinted from *Marriage*, September, 1967, in *New Dynamics in Sexual Love, Ibid.*).

Much has been said and written about sexual impotence and frigidity in people. But these maladies are diagnosed in a way that is still quite unperceptive. Eventually it will be seen that desperation resulting from chastity and continence is symptomatic of a yet unrecognized depth of sexual impotence and frigidity in the human person. The inability to experience the act of *being love* without necessarily *making love* in a genital manner signifies impotence and frigidity in the deeper sexual powers. When genital sexuality is felt to be a *necessity* for physical and emotional health, it is certain that the person is either sexually immature, or deeply retarded in his psychosexual development.

As the human embryo emerges from something very simple into an organism that is fantastic for the minuteness of its complexity, the human body is differentiated. This process is meant to continue into the psychic and spiritual dimensions of human reality, but many persons become fixated below their potential. As sexuality becomes psychically and spiritually differentiated, the organic energy of sex is assimilated into the emotional-mental energy of sex, and the latter is assimilated into the spiritual dimension of human sexuality.

The person with a differentiated sexuality is able to experience sexual fulfillment in more than one kind of human action. The whole power of sexual energy is not invested in genital sexuality or in coital intercourse. In perceptive acts like seeing, listening and touching, and in the intimacies of conversing, kissing and embracing, *physical* sexual intercourse exists between husband and wife. In all these acts there is a union of body and spirit. In any one of them, sexual union may be just as *dynamic* as it is in coital intercourse, though not as *dramatic*. Human acts do not have to be dramatically physical in order to be physical.

Lying in the sun to acquire a good tan is just as physical as running a mile, though certainly in a different way. For deeply sexual persons, any form of sexual intercourse, such as sharing a loving and intimate dialogue is an end in itself and is not caught in a falling-domino relationship that must end in coitus in order to be completely heterosexual. The insistence that sexual union must always include genitality shows a lack of sexual differentiation, and is a symptom of fixation in an early stage of psychosexual development. The fixated person may be very capable of genital functioning, but if his sexuality is compulsively genital, he is sexually retarded and congested, and lacks the dynamism of a deeper sexual life.

Coital intercourse is good, it is widely claimed, because the body is good. But the goodness of the body is often limited to its functional goodness alone. The body is judged to be good because it is *good for something;* in this case, it is useful for love and pleasure. From the viewpoint of the functionalist, unused sexual organs imply a denial of their goodness. But the human body is good, first of all, because of its primary value as an internal revelation of the person's being. An affirmation of the body that is limited to its functional goodness is a very subtle negation of the body, and so, of the whole person. An example of this sexual functionalism is the *Playboy* philosophy and practice. When it is thought that the flesh must be *worked* for everything one can get out of it, the Puritan work-ethic has fully penetrated the area of sexuality. Playboyism is Puritan functionalism transferred to an area of life where it was suppressed by the Puritans themselves.

Just as the Sabbath is a witness to the non-functional goodness of the world, non-functional sexuality may be a great witness to the goodness of the *being* of human sexuality. Thus, celibacy can be experienced as a celebration of the being of sex, or as a way of *being* one's sexuality without necessarily functioning in a coital way. Some organs of the body must, of necessity, fulfill their functional purpose if life is to continue. But the organs of man's sexuality exist in his being as a special revelation of his freedom. Even in marriage, it is possible to experience the being of sexual love without necessarily, though freely, making love. The way to the fullness of sexual joy is not *necessarily* through the fullness of sexual passion and pleasure. At its best, mental-emotional health and vigor is marked by a strong sexual interiority.

There are two basic powers in man and woman for full sexual union in marriage. One is the power for the coital act; the other is the more indirect power for sexual communion in any of their acts of sharing. Until now, however, the direct relationship of coitus has been the only form of relationship admitted to be a consummation of human sexuality. But the indirect relationship of communion is also structured in the metaphysical depths of human sexuality. (For an in-depth description of this more indirect way of sexual consummation, see *New Dynamics in Sexual Love, ibid.*)

Since the metaphysical dimension of the human body transcends, while fully animating and including, its physical dimension, and is the origin within the person of his physical sexuality, there is a metaphysical union of two in one flesh as well as a physical union. As the persons become sexually differentiated together, this deeper union may become more and more strengthened and all-pervading. Then they easily realize, that the way to sexual joy in body and in spirit together, is not *necessarily* through sexual passion and pleasure.

Actually, sexual fulfillment is more indirect than direct by its very nature. This is true because sexual fulfillment is a feeling of peace with oneself. If a person lacks this sense of inner peace with himself, no amount of coital activity with another person will make him sexually fulfilled. Sexual fulfillment begins before birth in the unspoken relation between the child and his mother. Recently, there is scientific evidence that the baby develops an attitude toward himself already in his mother's womb. Part of the explanation for this phenomenon is the manner in which psychic states in the mother affect chemical processes. Furthermore, nonverbal communication is powerful in all human relationships. And when one human being actually inhabits the being of another, as is the case with pregnancy, nonverbal human communication through attitudes and feelings must be a truly dynamic reality.

The sexual fulfillment that begins in the relation between mother and child before birth continues in childhood and adolescence into adulthood through the love of parents, siblings, teachers, neighbors and friends. And this fulfillment takes place whether there is any coital experience or not. It is therefore possible for celibacy to be a sign of deep sexual fulfillment. And a considerable degree of this basic sexual fulfillment is actually a prerequisite for a good coital relationship. If coital intercourse takes place before this readiness exists, it tends to retard sexual development, and fixation may result. Thereafter, the person feels a constant need to seek sexual fulfillment through genitality, but a limitless amount of coital passion and pleasure will not increase sexual fulfillment unless this fulfillment is relatively advanced before a coital relationship begins.

Other examples of premature activity resulting in retarded growth appear in the life of primitive peoples. In some tribes, children manage their own canoes by the time they are five years old. Sometimes, three and four-year-olds make traps and learn to use them for catching animals. But the price that is paid by all forced growth is fixation at an early age. If the almost unlimited capacity of human beings for growth is to be protected and encouraged to develop, forced growth through premature activities must be avoided. And one of the most common of all premature activities is genital activity resulting in the phallic fixation that besets the lives of so many people.

The coital act is the most dramatic of all forms of human

communication. It has much in common with other forms of communication, but, at the same time, it remains a special kind of communication, having the greatest amount of involvement and complexity. People may meet, share a conversation, then depart and never see one another again. But when such a coming and going exists in coital relationships, it is a matter of promiscuity or prostitution. Animals may come and go in copulating with one another, but human sexuality is so different from animal sexuality that a similar behavior in humans must be considered malfunctional. Even in speaking, there are some things we reveal only to our most intimate friends. Coital communication is meant to be a still more concentrated sharing, a revelation only to, and with, one other person. Ordinarily, we cannot sustain without chaos a form of communication so dramatic and complex with more than one other person. And if this form of communication is made to become less complex, or if it is treated as just a casual and passing affair, it is profoundly depersonalized.

The human power for the coital act is like a tree that extends its roots into all the other powers of human life and being. Before the person is ready for such an intimate and extroverted involvement with another person, the other powers of his being need to be developed enough to provide a good ground for the expansive roots of the coital power. The most involving of human communications should have a large and well-developed context in other forms of communication, otherwise it is premature.

Again, the coital act is like the peak of a mountain with the largest and broadest part of the mountain supporting this peak. Before two persons are ready to become so dramatic about each other, or to share the coital form of communication, they need to broaden the base of this interaction by sharing all other ways of living together, and this includes the marriage commitment and the sharing of a home.

Just as the act of listening begins in the mind and spirit

while assimilating the physical organs of hearing, the coital act is meant to begin in the mind and spirit of love while assimilating the impulses and physical organs of sexuality. In this way, the coital union is a sublimated, fully humanized form of behavior. It is based in human freedom and love rather than in a physiological reflex. Without compulsion and necessity, coital intercourse is neither lust nor luxury, but one among many forms of expressing human love and freedom.

Chapter 11

TWO IN ONE FLESH

For the Hebrews, the first to use the expression "two in one flesh" to describe to union of marriage, flesh was not just the physical body, but the entire person and his relatives and belongings. The members of a kinship group had one flesh, a collective reality belonging to all. When a woman married, she became a member of her husband's family. By entering his kinship group she was thought to become one flesh with her husband. This idea is continued in our culture today, and is the reason that a woman takes her husband's family name. Thus, the original idea of two in one flesh was that of a corporate reality as extensive as the husband's family. That the unity of flesh is based in the husband's family rather than in the family of his wife was in harmony with the origin of woman from man, Eve from Adam.

In his epistle to the Ephesians, St. Paul continues this idea of a whole community in *one flesh*, and describes sacramental marriage by comparing the relationship between husband and wife to the relationship between Christ and his Church. In saying that we are members of Christ's body, "made from his flesh and from his bones" (Eph 5-30), he does not mean that we are made physically from his flesh and bones, but that we are, in another way, all *one flesh* in Christ. The meaning is basically communal rather than anatomical. Then reference is made to *Genesis* where Adam called Eve "bone of my bones and flesh of my flesh." But Adam was not speaking of skeletal bone or muscular flesh. In this revelation about the nature of marriage, bone and flesh are not to be interpreted primarily in a physical way, but in another more communal way that transcends, while including, the physical. Thus, besides the physical meaning of two in one flesh, there is also a metaphysical meaning, or a mystical meaning in the Christian sense. A man and a woman become two in one flesh in a way that is more mysterious, yet more essential and dynamic, than has commonly been thought. Perhaps this is why St. Paul exclaimed, in describing the Chistian sacrament of two in one flesh, "This is a great mystery."

It has been taken for granted that a man and woman become two in one flesh only in the coital embrace. But the reality of two in one flesh exists primarily in the covenant of marriage, an act of the whole person through his will, and in the context of kinship, friends and the wider society of the world. This is the first consummation of marriage, and it remains a consummation, a union of two in one flesh, whether or not the persons ever choose a coital expression of their union. In and through this original and abiding consummation, all their acts of sharing, even the most daily and ordinary, become marriage-acts. Why shouldn't there be more than one way of body-spirit conjugal union? Thus, the celibate union of Joseph and Mary was a union of two in one flesh.

The sexuality of the person in his flesh is intuitive, or perceptive, as well as directly functional. The dynamic act of *being love* is just as sexual as the more functional act of *making love* in a genital manner. In fact, the abiding attitude of being love is meant to be dynamic in all acts of expressing love, whether genital or not. The most dramatic of these acts is coital intercourse. But the most dramatic expression is not necessary for fulfillment in sexual activity just as the most dramatic act of reasoning in a complexly technical analysis is not necessary for fulfillment in mental activity. In and through the intuitive, or metaphysical, dimension of the flesh, it is possible to experience a deep and consummating heterosexual and conjugal communion that is truly dynamic without necessarily involving the most dramatic form of interpersonal communication.

As the human intellect is both intuitive and rationally functional in its modes of knowing, with different degrees of mutuality between these modes, human sexuality is both intuitive and functional in its modes of loving. As the intuitive union of the human intellect with the world may be a complete union of knowing, the intuitive union of a man and woman with each other may be a complete union of loving. But functional acts of *making love*, whether genital or not, without a strong basis in the intuitive act of *being love*, are as incomplete as the act of reasoning without intuitive presence.

Because the deeper, more beingful experience of two in one flesh is so undeveloped in people, they are forced to become not only desperate with periodic continence, but also incredulous toward the truly natural possibility for conjugal celibacy. Married people who find continence — a result of being love without necessarily making love in a genital manner — a separating, or tension-producing experience, need to become two in one flesh more dynamically than they are.

The idea that a long period of continence is a way of living in marriage like a brother and sister is unreflective and deeply mistaken. Because every act of sharing by married persons is a marriage-act, it is impossible for a loving husband and wife to share these acts simply with a brother-sister quality. Between married persons, a kiss, a smile or a conversation is qualitatively different than a kiss, a smile or a conversation between a brother and his sister, or between any other man and woman not married to each other. Nor is a conjugal relationship, even in periods of continence, meant to be a "platonic" relationship. Originally, "platonic friendship" meant a homosexual relation between males, and is therefore falsely applied to any man-woman relationship. Friendship is a strong and rich basis for conjugal love.

But friendship in marriage is always marital and deeply special in its heterosexual intimacy.

In the marriage of Christ and his Church, all Christians are united in one flesh and married to one another. Still more basically, all beings in the world are united in the marriage of creation. In this broad and most basic sense of marriage, a man and woman are one flesh before their communal witness consummates their union in spousal marriage. Still, there is as much difference between these dimensions of marriage as between the union of ovum and sperm before and after the beginning of a new person. In some real sense, spousal marriage is the beginning of a new person that a man and a woman become together. And once this "new person" begins, divorce is as metaphysically impossible as separating a zygote into ovum and sperm is physically impossible once they are expressly united.

Currently there is a strong tendency to think that a marriage must be psychologically harmonious or it may not even be a marriage. But this is like thinking that a person must be psychologically adequate or he may not even be a person. (The fallacy of psychologism.) Just as a person may be physically, emotionally or spiritually crippled while remaining a person, a marriage may be physically, emotionally or spiritually disturbed while remaining a marriage. Divorce may be physically and morally attempted, as it often is, but what God has united, in and through the truthfully expressed covenant of a man and a woman, they themselves are metaphysically incapable of separating. Just as the person does not have to be fully grown to be a person, a marriage does not have to be fully developed to be a marriage; it may exist even in an embryonic state of psychic union.

In some real sense, then, the unity of two persons in one flesh is as complete as the unity of the person's being that survives even death. Divorce may be the result of a kind of psychic and moral death in a marrige, but the most basic unity of marriage survives even this death. The meaning of two in one flesh is not only physical, psychological, social and moral, but most fundamentally of all, it is ontodynamic, or based in the dynamics of being.

Chapter 12

CONTRACEPTION AND THE
SACRAMENT OF MARRIAGE

As a sacrament of the Church, marriage is a special relationship of human nature to divine grace, and of divine grace to human nature. "By virtue of this sacrament, as spouses fulfill their conjugal and family obligation, they are penetrated with the spirit of Christ, which suffuses their whole lives with faith, hope and charity." (Vatican II, *The Church in the Modern World*, Section on Marriage and the Family.) The sacramental grace of marital union enlarges, strengthens and deepens the natural grace of this union.

Because the entire reality of two persons and all their actions participate in the sacrament of marriage, there is a sacramental, as well as a natural, union between the coital act and its generative power, just as there is a sacramental and natural union between the spouses themselves. Even ovulation and spermatogenesis, by participation, are sacramental, as well as natural, movements of being. In both the relationships between husband and wife, and between their coital union and its generative power, the grace of the sacrament enlarges, strengthens and deepens the grace of nature. Indeed, *it has been largely for sacramental reasons that the Church has been so intently concerned about the natural integrity of human sexuality in all its aspects.* If the human nature of the person's sexuality is not fully sustained, the very ground and environment of the sacrament is undermined.

As a sacramental way of life, marriage is not totally subject to the value judgments of the individual. All the sacraments are subject to the value judgments of the Church. And the document of Vatican II on marriage insists that "sons of the Church may not undertake methods of birth control which are found blameworthy by the teaching authority of the Church in its unfolding of the divine law." Other areas of life, such as state government and education, are not directly related to this authority, the Magisterium; they are not sacraments of the Church, as is marriage.

It is true that the authority of the Church exists in the people as well as in the Pope. But these are two different kinds of authority. Just as there is a real distinction, not a separation, between Christ and the Church, there is a real difference between the Magisterium and the Church as a community. Though the Pope is not Christ, his Office exists as a special relationship with Christ. The authority of his Office partly transcends the authority in the community, and would not be finally bound by a consensus within this community. Even the president in a democracy is meant to be a leader and not just a passive follower of the people. He has the power to veto certain proposals of the legislative body. And the Church is not meant to be a democracy any more than it is meant to be an absolute monarchy. Christ's call to the perfection of love and being is something much more than the common good in a democratic society.

Jesus did not always consult his apostles or the majority of his followers in making his decisions. When he said that he would give them his body to eat and his blood to drink, the disciples were shocked. "This is a hard saying," they remarked. "Who can listen to it?" Then the gospel tells us that many of them walked with Jesus no longer. But he did not change his teaching to win their acceptance; he acted independently, though respectfully.

To the extent that Pope Paul acted independently, he was not unjustified. But his independence was only partial. He did not agree with the majority of his commission, but he did agree with the basic implications in the Council's document on marriage. This document, though it contains no mention of contraception by name, carries within it strong implications against contraception, while expressing, also, a sincere recognition of the problems of family size and birth regulation. In his encyclical on *Human Life*, Pope Paul quoted from this consensus of the bishops, "a true contradiction cannot exist between the Divine laws pertaining to the transmission of life and those pertaining to the fostering of authentic conjugal love," a statement of the principle of inseparability. Furthermore, abortion is mentioned by the Council as the most extreme of the "dishonorable solutions," implying that there are other dishonorable practices.

The Council also maintained that the human generative power surpasses the reproductive power of animals, and that it may not be treated as a simply biological power in ways allowable for the animals. "The sexual characteristics of man and the human power of generation go astonishingly beyond those which belong to lower forms of life." In his encyclical, Pope Paul continued this idea by saying that the human generative power must be treated as a part of the person (# 10).

According to the Council: "When there is a question of harmonizing conjugal love with the responsible transmission of life, the moral aspect of any procedure does not depend solely on sincere intention or on an evaluation of motives, but must be determined by objective standards." This means that the individual conscience is not the source of morality. Some of the post-encyclical pastorals seemed to intimate that conscience may be a source of morality in this matter. If this is actually the case these bishops contradicted their conciliar statement, and this contradiction, if it exists, would have to be rectified eventually.

In stating the source of morality, a direct reference is made by the Council's document to the traditionally affirmed basis of the natural law: "the nature of the human person and his acts." Nothing is said about interpreting "the nature of the human person and his acts" in the light of contemporary theology, though this may have been intended by some of those who formulated the Council's statement. But it need not have been intended by the Council as a whole, since the contemporary or psychologistic frame of reference for interpreting the natural law is not mentioned in the document. Pope Paul was left free to choose the traditional frame of reference for understanding "the nature of the human person and his acts"— which he did.

According to the Council, the objective standards of morality that follow from the nature of the human person and his acts "preserve the full sense of mutual self-giving and human procreation in the context of true love." What is the *full* sense of procreation, as well as of mutual self-giving? Pope Paul interpreted the full sense of procreation to be the openness of every conjugal act to procreation unless the generative power were naturally inactive. And he interpreted the *full* sense of mutual self-giving to include personal sacrifice based on mutual respect for the *whole person* including his generative power. The Council's document offers a powerful clue for this interpretation. This full sense of both procreation and self-giving is based on chastity. "Such a goal cannot be achieved unless the virtue of conjugal chastity is sincerely practiced." Both the conjugal expression of love and the transmission of life are regulated by chastity. This deeply implies that conjugal chastity is the basis of the harmony between mutual self-giving and procreation, without which an inauthentic contradiction begins to appear.

If husbands are related to their wives as Christ is related to his Church (Eph 5:21-33), they do not find in Christ's relation with his Church a similitude for contraception. The life-giving grace of Christ flows into the womb of the Church, his bride and spouse, to conceive new life in Baptism and to sustain this new life in the other sacraments. Christ is not contraceptive in relation to his Church, nor is the Church, in her exercise of the sacraments, contraceptive in her relation to Christ. Individuals, however, can refuse the reception of grace within the very act of the sacrament. Withholding, or lying in the sacrament of reconciliation, renders the confession sacrilegious. As a sacramental act, the coital union of husband and wife may also be rendered sacrilegious.

Instead of inventing contraceptives for woman, instead of urging her to use them or forcing her into a situation which tempts her to resort to their use, instead of using them himself in his relation to her, a man ought to lay down his life in sacrifice, as Christ laid down his life for his Church.

> Husbands, love your wives, just as Christ also loved the Church, and delivered himself up for her . . . in order that he might present to himself the Church in all her glory, not having spot or wrinkle or any such thing, but that she might be holy and without blemish (Eph 5:25-7).

If, on the other hand, it is the wife who desires contraception, she is in need of strength from her husband, as the Church receives light and strength from Christ. No sacrament of the Church allows for an interference in natural processes that participate in the sacrament.

Sacraments other than the Eucharist are marked by hard sayings and difficult meanings. Nicodemus was dismayed when Jesus said that unless a man be born again he cannot enter the kingdom of God. The Scribes were horrified when Jesus told the paralytic that his sins were forgiven. Yet he gave this power to men with the words, "whose sins you shall forgive, they are forgiven; and whose sins you shall retain, they are retained." The Pharisees were being obnoxious when they asked Jesus whether it was lawful for a man to put away his wife; the law of Moses had allowed divorce. But Jesus said this was due to the hardness of the people's hearts. "What God has united, let no one separate." His disciples were disturbed by these difficult words, and they began to ask him their meaning.

If we believe and hold that marriage is an inseparable union of two persons, we are also called to believe and hold that marriage is an inseparable union of two interpersonal powers, the power for the conjugal act and its power for generating new life. However, if the marriage is invalid it may be dissolved; there is really no marriage to begin with. Similarly, in the case of rape, the use of contraceptives does not separate a coital act from its generative power because there is no coital act to begin with. The words of Jesus concerning the persons who marry, "what God has united, let no one separate," apply as much to the unity of these interpersonal powers as to the unity of persons, though in a different way. The word of the sacramental church on contraception, that it is a separation of realities united by God, not only in nature but also in sacrament, has become for these times a very hard saying, and one that is difficult to listen to. Many are turning away from it, but they take their leave of a powerfully personalized and Christian truth.

Chapter 13

SCRIPTURE AND TRADITION

Besides the above mentioned scriptural sources, which have implications about contraception, there is the story of Onan (Genesis 38:8-10). The act of Onan, coitus interruptus, or the coital act followed by withdrawal and ejaculation apart from coital union, is an act that is definable as contraceptive. Coitus interruptus is an internal separation of the coital act from its generative power. However, not all sexual acts with semination apart from coital union are contraceptive. Because no coital act or possibility for conception is involved, masturbation and homosexual acts are not contraceptive. These are forms of behavior that separate genital activity from coital union, rather than separating coital union from its generative power. But coitus interruptus has the same meaning as semination in a condom, though the biological locus of semination and the manner of terminating the coital act make it different. Since contraception is not defined by biological locus, nor by the way in which an ejaculatory coital act is terminated, these differences do not distinguish the act of Onan from the definition of contraception.

According to the levirate law, a man was to beget children with a dead brother's widow so that the dead brother's name would not vanish from Israel (Deuteronomy 25:5-10). At the bidding of his father, Onan married Thamar, his brother's widow. And knowing that any children born to them would not be his own, he spilled his seed on the ground every time he had intercourse with Thamar. This action was displeasing to Yahweh, God, and Onan was killed.

Some interpreters of the story say that Onan disobeyed his

father, that he broke the levirate law because of selfishness, and that his disobedience and selfishness, rather than his interruption of coitus, was displeasing to God. But an offender against this law, whether because of selfishness or any other reason, was not seriously punished by the levirate law itself. The widow was supposed to embarrass him in public (Dt 25:9). What, then, did Onan do to merit so severe a punishment? Had he avoided having intercourse with Thamar, would God have struck him dead? It does not seem that God would support a mere custom with so much authority. Only social custom can say that a dead man should have children conceived by his brother. But God knows that children of Onan conceived and fathered by him would actually be Onan's children. It seems much more proportionate that God's own law was disobeyed by the manner in which Onan prevented children from being conceived. Had he avoided having intercourse with Thamar, he would have disobeyed the levirate law, but not the law of God.

Though there is no other explicit mention in scriptural sources of a judgment on contraception, the profound emphasis of the Christian Testament on the value of virginity and celibacy was destined to predispose the Church, in its almost twenty centuries of tradition, to forbid contraception. The virginity of Jesus, his mother and Joseph, as well as the example of many Christians throughout the centuries, exists not only as an end in itself, but also as a sign of the basic virginity of being to which every Christian is called whether or not he marries and becomes a parent. In its broadest and most basic meaning, Christian virginity is the integrity of the whole person animated by love and charity. This meaning extends into marriage and is the very foundation of the sacrament, providing a strong sensitivity against anything that would violate the integrity of marriage in any of its acts. This universal dimension of Christian virginity has been the deepest animating force behind the long tradition of the Church's prohibition of practices such as contraception and divorce.

Furthermore, the deep scriptural reverence for human life has been a prohibitive force with regard to contraception and abortion. Though these practices are not explicitly condemned in the letter of scripture, they are condemned in its spirit. The absence of a direct statement in the letter of scripture does not mean its absence in the very substance of Christian revelation. And truths that are dynamic in the spirit of scripture often are expressed in the form of tradition.

Another example of a revealed truth carried by the tradition of the Church, and that is not explicit in the letter of scripture, though implied in its spirit, is the perpetual virginity of Mary. This truth is implicit in the virginal conception of Jesus, in the explicitly revealed celibacy of Mary and Joseph before the birth of Jesus (why before, if not after?), and in the fact that Jesus gave his mother to the care of John, as though there were no other sons or daughters to care for her. The tradition regarding contraception is as long as that regarding the virginity of Mary, and is similar in being related to the implicit revelation of scripture.

The importance of tradition may be strengthened in our minds when we realize that scripture itself was the written form of a tradition that sometimes preceded the writing by many years. And not all of this tradition was written down. This is why it is fundamentalistic to judge revelation by the letter of scripture alone, and not also by its unwritten spirit.

But the traditional teaching on contraception is being challenged today, mostly because it is thought to have neither a scriptural foundation nor a real basis in the natural law. The deep substance of both is not being perceived. Besides misunderstanding the teaching of scripture on contraception, contemporary scholars have falsely identified the articulated tradition of the Church with its real tradition. The articulated tradition, particularly in some of the Fathers of the Church, is so obviously limited by a biologistic and primitive knowledge of the coital act and its generative power that the recent criticism is necessary. Most of Christian history has lacked a philosophy and theology of Christian marriage. And what there was of it (from St. Augustine for example) has been misunderstood. Laws have outdistanced meanings to such an extent that the laws have been losing their value. Without a rich and deeply inspiring meaning for marriage, laws of marriage must eventually become questioned, and even denied, out of sheer frustration. But these serious faults in the expressed tradition of the Church are not to be identified with the unexpressed, more intuitive and real tradition.

The present movement toward a positive philosophy and theology of human sexuality in marriage is a sign of new life in developing the real tradition of the Church. By valuing equally the love of spouses for each other and their procreation of children, Vatican II progressed beyond *Casti Connubii*. But this affirmation of equality between the two meanings of the conjugal act does not imply an acceptance of contraception. When Vatican II abandoned the old argument that the primary purpose of marriage is procreation, it was immediately thought that a change in the previous view about contraception was implied. The assertion of equality between conjugal love and procreation was, indeed, an advancement beyond the previous position about primary and secondary ends of marriage. But contrary to widespread expectations, it was actually a strengthening, not a weakening, of the grounds for opposing contraception.

The weakness of criticizing contraception because it goes against the primary purpose of a human act may be seen when we stop to realize that the basic, if not only, purpose of animal copulation is reproduction. Yet, this is not a reason for opposing the sterilization of animals. A man does not think it immoral to separate copulation and reproduction by sterilizing or other means, any more than he thinks it immoral to kill animals for food. But the conjugal act is much more than copulation, and its fruitfulness in new life is much more than reproduction. The unitive and generative values of the conjugal act raise it above the separability of copulation and reproduction. Where a man will kill animals for food, he will not kill other persons for food, even when he is starving to death. The essential difference in what may be done to animals and to persons applies with still greater meaning in the area of sexuality, because the conjugal act is not necessary for individual survival as is the eating of food.

But, though the document of Vatican II on marriage is an advancement from *Casti Connubii,* it offers no really insightful discoveries to help couples interpret the deeper dynamism of their sexuality. And the recent encyclical on celibacy still upholds celibacy as something negative for the sake of something positive. Eventually, as the evolution of insight progresses, celibacy will be seen as a positively creative fulfillment of human sexuality in its broader dimension. And new possibilities for sexuality in marriage will be revealed. But this evolution will depend upon the development of a new metaphysics of human reality. In order to refine the tradition of the Church, theology needs a developing and more radical philosophy of being to fulfill its mission of articulating the faith.

Theology depends as much upon the philosophy of being as it depends upon faith. Without an adequate metaphysics, theology simply cannot exist and grow as an articulation of faith. This is why the traditional articulation of the nature of contraception has been so poor. A metaphysics of human nature with a biological frame of reference has little to offer a theology that is grounded in faith. In the intuitive life of the Church, the evil of contraception has always been vitally felt and darkly understood, but no way to adequately explain this intuition has existed.

Here especially, we must be careful to distinguish the real dynamism of tradition in the Church from the faulty and groping articulation of this tradition. If the explanation has been poor, this does not mean that the tradition itself must be abandoned.

The real tradition of the Church on contraception, and one that permeates the Magisterium, is a beingful intuition enlightened by divine revelation and faith. And this real tradition has existed in the Church like the largest part of an island below the surface of its articulation.

But most Christians today, and many theologians, do not seem to have this intuition about contraception. It is being repressed and denied in the face of many almost overwhelming pressures. A recognition of the poverty of the traditional articulation on contraception, and a false identification of this articulation with the real tradition itself, besides the population crisis with its demand for immediate solutions, are all working against the real tradition.

Yet in trying to justify contraception, critics of the tradition have been reinforcing the old crudity of biologism in their interpretation of the human generative power. While contemporary theologians are emphasizing the sacramentality of the coital act in marriage, they are biologizing its generative power more than ever. Consequently, the separatism insinuated between the coital act and its generative power widens and deepens. But the sacramentality of the human generative power is *equal* with the sacramentality of the coital act. This equality of sacramental value is strongly implied in the views of Vatican II on the nature and meaning of Christian marriage, and is fully affirmed in the encyclical on *Human Life*.

But we must wonder why the Catholic church, particularly in its magisterial center, is the only Christian church that so insistently opposes contraception. Other Christians have become fundamentalists on this issue. They have reasoned as follows: the Bible does not say word for word that contraception is wrong, therefore it can be right. And now, many Catholic theologians are thinking in the same fundamentalist manner. But the authentic Catholic mentality is more complex than this. If scripture does not say explicitly that contraception is wrong, it is immediately realized that scripture does not say contraception is, or can be, right. Therefore it might be wrong. As a result, other sources of revelation need to be consulted.

Catholic Christianity is based on three sources of revelation instead of scripture alone. Along with scripture — tradition and the natural being of God's creation are regarded as sources of divine revelation. When it is clearly realized that scripture was originally an oral tradition of a good number of years before this tradition was only partially written, tradition is valued as a very important source of revelation. And the interest of Catholic Christianity in the natural law is due to a strong sense of revelation in natural being. This complex sense of revelation needs to be sustained, even in the face of the many pressures that militate against it.

The one form of birth regulation allowed by the Church is noticeable for the complexity that it involves and affirms. But it is a complexity proportionate to the richness of aspects in the unity of man and woman. According to Teilhard de Chardin, the progress of evolution is a process of centration in complexification. An authentic sense of complexity, and resistance to over-simplification, is therefore necessary for the development of Christianity. Thus, the Catholic form of Christianity, with its three sources of revelation, has a vitally important mission to the future.

4

Chapter 14

INCREASE AND FILL THE EARTH – A CRISIS

Whatever might be said about the meaning of contraception in the light of nature and sacrament, or scripture and tradition, the potential, if not yet fully actual, population crisis of the earth forces itself upon us and seems to demand a contraceptive solution. It is not enough to think in terms of opening up more land and more potential sources of food. Man does not live by bread alone, but also by the other good things of the earth including its wide open spaces and areas of solitude and wilderness. Furthermore, the rate of human population growth must be slowed down because the planet is simply not large enough to sustain this rate of expansion indefinitely. Though contraception may be viewed as the simplest and most efficient "solution" to the population crisis, this problem is a challenge as complex as our being and our relation with the earth. Such a complex challenge cannot have a simple solution.

Perhaps the readiness to look for a simple way to curb the multiplication of people follows from the simple way in which the ancient blessing to "increase and multiply and fill the earth" has always been received. But there is more than one way for man and woman to receive this blessing of their sexuality. They were created to fill the earth not only in a procreative way, but also in a co-creative way. This is what St. Paul intimates when he says that "the eager longing of creation awaits the revelation of the sons of God" (Romans 8:19). Man and woman are called to fill the earth, not only with others of their kind, but with love for the very being of the world. Through their co-creative love for the world, they are meant to participate in the "new creation" and gradually to co-create, together with God, the

"new earth" that is foretold in *Revelation* (21:1). For this fulfillment, as St. Paul says, "all creation groans and travails in
pain."

In considering the intimate relationship of man and woman
with the earth, its limited size in relation to the human generative potential must be regarded as significant. Their calling
to receive and co-create the earth is also an invitation to receive
its limited space in a co-creative manner. Shall they respond
to this calling by inserting all kinds of stoppers into their generative power? The limited size of the planet, in relation to the
human generative potential, is an invitation to man and woman
to evolve in a true kind of sexual freedom, "because creation
itself also will be delivered from its slavery to corruption into
the freedom of glory of the sons of God" (Romans 8:21). Between a husband and wife, this freedom is the ability to experience the fulfillment of being love without *necessarily* making
love in a genital manner. Toward this evolution in freedom,
Pope Paul's encyclical on *Human Life* is both an invitation and
a challenge. (Cf., "The Evolution of Love," by Mary R. Joyce,
Insight, Winter, 1968. See Appendix).

As the relationship between man and woman evolves, their
sexuality becomes less and less grounded in necessity, and more
fulfilled in freedom. They become capable of realizing the
co-creative, as well as the procreative, blessing of marriage. And,
as their procreative vocation becomes more fulfilled in their
relation with the earth, other aspects of their co-creative vocation become increasingly more important.

But people must be prepared for this inevitable transition
in their sexual vocation. Unless they are able to understand
themselves in depth, and the immense possibilities for sexual
differentiation, they cannot assimilate their sexual powers in a
fully human way. Understanding is the condition for assimilation.
Man's sexuality cannot become fully human, fully assimilated,
without a continuing education that explores the beingful, as

well as the psychic and physical dimensions of human sexual energy. Education toward the deeper fulfillment and freedom of human sexuality is the most creative response that can be given to the crisis in filling the earth.

But education is not enough. It must be supported and implemented by scientific research of the kind that will enable people to regulate conception by assimilating rather than separating the relation of the coital act and its generative power. Because the method of regulating conception by periodic continence is based on the principle of assimilation rather than on internal separation, it is a fully human response to the need for limiting the population of the earth. Scientific research is therefore urgently needed to find a way of implementing this human principle of assimilation as it relates to the art of regulating conception. Together with education toward an in-depth kind of sexual freedom, this blessing of science would enable man and woman to assimilate, rather than to overpopulate, the earth.

In the meantime, many people are employing crisis-solutions to critical situations. We must hope that these solutions are being carefully evaluated. When a person thinks that he is being forced to choose between evils, he should not think that one of these evils is as good as the other. The manslaughter of abortion is a greater evil than contraception. So-called contraceptives that are really abortifacients should be evaluated as qualitatively different from other contraceptives. The possibility that the anovulant pill may be aborting in many cases, particularly when the dosage is low, makes it even more questionable than the diaphragm or condom. Between contraception and abortion there is yet another alternative that must be preferred to abortion. Through permanent sterilization the person deforms himself instead of killing another.

Still, after all is said and done, the reality of human generation, the beginning of the person's existence without which there is nothing else, is the very ground and center of all human values. When the human generative power is no longer deeply respected, all other human values begin to be undermined.

And when children are regarded as either wanted or unwanted in a utilitarian manner, they are no longer so readily received as gifts. The child who is received as a gift is much more than wanted, and is not in danger of becoming unwanted. The merely wanted child, on the other hand, easily may be regarded as a possession similar to property or things, and readily may become unwanted if certain conditions of life are changed. Furthermore, it is easy to begin thinking that children have no right to exist when they are unwanted. Thus, abortion or neglect easily become ways of reacting against the unwanted child.

Can we begin to imagine the deep and subtle psychic damage done to children born in a world where adults are judging them as wanted or unwanted possessions? We are not yet aware of the subconscious knowledge that children have of their parents attitudes, and of the long-range effects of this subconscious perception. Thus, the ancient blessing, "ever ancient, ever new," to increase and fill the earth with life and love has tremendously complex and challenging implications, and must be carefully and thoughtfully received.

Chapter 15

THE BASIS OF MORALITY IN BEING

Today's new morality is not new enough. It is seriously lagging behind the deepest demands of the times. Not until we begin to think about our attitudes and behavior in much more radical terms will a really new morality be forthcoming. Previously, moral questions such as that of contraception were answered in terms of biological or pre-Freudian interpretations of psychic nature. Now the same questions are being answered in the context of psycho-sociological situations. But neither the bio-psychic nor the situational emphasis confronts the very ground of moral *being*.

The philosophy of being, metaphysics, is a way of thinking about reality by asking the question — "why is there anything rather than nothing at all?" In any area of interest, including morality, metaphysical thinking moves in and through the light of this most radical of questions.

Underlying the first of the specifically moral questions, "what shall I do?" is the beingful question, "why do I exist?" Apparently, it makes no difference to a piece of granite, or a pine tree or a squirrel, that it is something rather than nothing. These creatures cannot be awed or moved by the fact of their existence. But man can become aware of his being. Of all creatures of nature, he alone can ask the question, "why do I exist?"

In creating a being capable of knowing that he exists, God was asking of this creature something he could ask of no other. A *response* to the gift of being; responsibility. This call for a response to being is the origin of morality in being. But, have we responded well? Somehow, in some primordial way, we have not responded with unreserved gratitude. We have not received our being as fully as it was given. We have not rejoiced to be ourselves. Sometimes people say with defiance, "I did not ask to be created." These words really mean, "I did not receive my being."

Our Creator wills our reality to be out of nothingness, but we are created to share in our own creation by actively receiving the gift of being as fully as it is given. We are called to co-create ourselves together with God. But we have responded to being with hesitation, with doubt, with a lack of trust and faith. TO BE OR NOT TO BE. That is the most basic moral question. These immortal words of Hamlet reflect something in the depths of every human being.

We are responsible for our failure to receive our own being, a state of neglect out of which our daily failures originate. This state of neglect in receiving the deep unity of our being is the original failure of our lives. Whatever might be meant by original sin, it has something to do with our coming into being out of nothingness, and falling back again toward the nothingness from which we came. Any intensive study of anxiety reveals it as a dread of nothingness that is much more than an emotional or psychic reaction. Philosophers like Kierkegaard, Heidegger, Tillich and Sartre have identified the sense of nothingness at the bottom of man's anxiety, resulting in a dread of nothingness that is more a state of being than a psychic neurosis. They have called this deeper disturbance "existential" or existence anxiety.

Man's failure to become responsible for his being by fully receiving the gift of himself, results in a tension between being and nothingness in the depths of his being. In the relation between being and nothingness, he also encounters the relation between good and evil. The good is being, and the evil is the fall of being toward the nothingness from which being is created. In hesitating to receive his reality as fully as it given, man experiences a partial return to nothingness, and finds himself caught in a tension between being and nothingness. In ordinary life, this most basic state of existence is manifested in the tension between joy and sorrow, health and sickness, love and hatred, life and death.

In these days of situation ethics, it is understandable that some theologians are interpreting original sin in terms of the sociological situation into which we are born. There is no doubt that the reality of original sin has a sociological dimension, but even more importantly, it has an ontological basis. Original sin is not primarily a sociological situation *into which* man is born, but a condition of being *with which* he is born. If the child came into this world untouched by sin, he would not so readily absorb the distortions and errors in his environment, nor so unwittingly make them his own.

Man's original failure in the face of being, a condition with which he is born, in some mysterious sense, transcends both heredity and environment. This is true because man's relation with being transcends, while deeply including, his genetic inheritance and life surroundings. This much is revealed in *Genesis*, that man's very nature participates in this most basic failure, the failure to receive being. Adam, meaning everyman, is responsible. In other words, each human person is responsible for his failure to BE himself.

But why do we hesitate to receive the gift of being? Somehow, we do not want to be the kind of being that we are, finite rather than infinite. We do not fully accept our finitude. In doubting the value of our finite being we have fallen back again toward nothingness into sickness, anxiety, sin and death.

In our hesitation to receive our finite being, there is not only a lack of trust in God and an element of self-negation; there is also fear. A fear of nothingness. Like a child afraid of the darkness and running to his father as a refuge, we are afraid of the nothingness from which we came. There is an element of pathos in our failure to be. But fear brings on the very thing that is feared. In being afraid of nothingness by fearing our finitude, we fall back again toward nothingness, partly being and partly not being. And in our eagerness to escape this profound condition, we forget our original fear so that it is submerged in the form of a deep ontological anxiety as a reaction to something unknown or no longer remembered.

Our original fear of nothingness is like the fear of Peter walking on water. When he began to hesitate, or to turn his attention away from Jesus toward the water beneath his feet, he began to experience the very thing he feared. Peter falling toward the water is a great existential symbol of every man in his primordial fall toward nothingness. And Peter being lifted up again by the power of his Savior is a sign of man's salvation.

We are able to overcome the fall of our being toward nothingness by deeply and responsibly *receiving* the gift of being. The first imperative is BE! This is the basis of all other moral imperatives. Be-ing is the act of all our acts. Talking, walking, thinking, speaking and writing are ways of be-ing. The most basic kind of doing is be-ing. And be-ing is something that we are called to *do*. This is the basis of morality in being.

In the most basic sense of morality, to do *good* is to receive our being as consciously and as fully as possible. And, in the most basic sense, to do evil is to fail to receive our being. The primary moral act is one of receiving. Every other moral act is a particular way of receiving being. The primary immoral act is one of failing to receive being. And every other immoral act is a particular way of failing to be. Receiving is not passive, but is "more active than all active things." Receiving is a co-creative act. A failure to receive being generates taking, a substitute for receiving.

The first imperative of morality, that we receive our own being, implies a readiness to receive the being of other persons, the world and God. This attitude and act of receiving is the most basic meaning of love. We are called to love ourselves because it is good to be, to love the world because it IS, to love God because God IS. Morality will fail when we do not love by receiving being. Love means receiving more basically than it means giving. The best way to give oneself to another is to receive that person in his very being. (Part of the material in this chapter is taken from "To Be Something and Not Nothing," by Mary R. Joyce, *Marriage*, June, 1968.)

Chapter 16

LOVE, LAW AND SITUATION IN MORALITY

Because of the importance of be-ing in morality, the act of receiving being, as an act of love, is fundamental. Love is the basic dynamism of the fully moral act. But love is not enough. Recently, there has been a strong tendency in thinking about morality to assert that love is enough and that law is unnecessary. This is like saying that to be a man the spirit is enough and the body is unnecessary. Previously, people thought about human nature in terms of body and soul as if these were separate entities. But now, the unity of the person is newly affirmed. A similar sense of complexity in unity must be affirmed of the moral act. As spirit and body are intrinsically united in the human person, love and law are intrinsically united in the human act. An ethics that recognizes only love, or that overemphasizes the importance of love, is a kind of ethical spiritualism.

Though love is the dynamic spirit of moral actions, it must be as differentiated as the variety of moral actions themselves. As there are many different kinds of moral actions, there are many different ways of manifesting love. The first imperative of morality, that we receive our being, generates another imperative related to the act of speaking, that we receive our power to speak as a power to express our minds both to ourselves and to others. This implies the good of truthfulness and the evil of lying. To do good and to avoid evil in human communication is marked by the law of truthfulness. And this law is a particular differentiation of love as the act of receiving the gift of being. Love is expressed in truthfulness and denied in lying.

Besides speaking, there are many other ways for a human person to act or to refuse to act. For each way there is a differentiation of love; there is a kind of good to affirm and evil to avoid. Just as an embryo is differentiated by many various but interrelated structures, love is differentiated by law. Love that is not differentiated by law is like an embryo that develops no internal structures and never becomes ready for birth and life. In the differentiation of love, or in and through moral laws, we learn how to do good and avoid evil so that we may receive our being in all we do in our daily lives. Had we never eaten of the "tree of knowledge of good and evil," it would not be necessary for us to develop projected codes of law as something separated from love. In the fullness of love for being, the laws of our nature would be fully integrated, and we would affirm these laws spontaneously just by love. We would not need to make these laws the objects of our concern, nor would we have to factor them out of our being so that we would know how to love. But now, in the darkness of our unknowing and unloving, we need to factor out the laws of our complex being as they become manifest to us not only by unaided reason but also by divine revelation. We need to know the laws of our being so that we may actively affirm its structures, thus having a guide to love in our most primordial act of receiving our being.

Love is the spirit of the law, but the structure of the law is the body of love. No man can affirm his spirit while he denies his body. In the moral dimension of life, no man can affirm love while he denies the structure of law. Nor can the body be affirmed while the spirit is denied. Similarly, to affirm the law while denying love is to misjudge the nature of the moral act.

An ethics of love must be finely and artistically integrated with law. People love many things — power, wealth, pleasure, social status, comfort etc., as well as the being of the things that are. Therefore, a love that is undifferentiated by law is dangerous. St. Augustine's idea: "love and do what you will," too readily becomes "do as you please and call it love."

Morality is like music; both are meant to be works of art. Both are meant to be a unity of spirit and structure. The person who dedicates his actions to the law without love is like the musician who performs his music with flawless technique but without the creative spirit of the music itself. Such a technician is not an artist. Another musician who is filled with the spirit and power of the music he performs, but who stumbles over and around its structures is even more intolerable than the technician. He is the more lovable for his spirit, but hardest on the ear. The real artist is both filled with the creative spirit of the music as well as a master of its structures in flawless technique. As each pianist who is an artist brings something unique to the same musical score, each brings something unique to the same structures of the moral law. We are not all called to become musical artists, but all are called to become artists in the moral life. Every person was created to eat of the "tree of life."

But we are not always capable of the full art of moral living. In many instances our power to love is minimal if not denied. For example, in the matter of civil rights, how many of us can say that we respond out of love? And, how many of us pay our taxes because of love? But a lack of love does not excuse us from moral response. Where love is lacking, justice takes over and becomes the ground of moral imperatives. We are commanded to do justice to others even though we may not love them. This is not the moral situation at its best, but at its least. In a sense, however, the imperatives of justice are imperatives of a minimal kind of love. A willingness to do justice to others is already a true degree of love.

The most basic laws that differentiate love and justice are the ten commandments and the natural law. In large part, the ten commandments imply the natural law. But they also imply the law of love to come with Christ. This explains their negative approach to morality. The "you shall nots" seem to be saying that it is not yet revealed what the fulless of moral life is, but it is revealed that the fullness of moral life *is not* in lying, stealing, commiting murder or adultery. This approach of negation is similar to the *via negativa* in our knowledge of God. We know God by negating about divine being what we actually know about finite being, then realizing that God is much more. Thus, we realize that God is a living being but that divine life is not a vegetative, sensient or human kind of life. With the coming of Christ and the law of love, the ten commandments were transformed into conditional or if-then imperatives. *If* you love your own being, the being of God and the being of your neighbor, *then* you will not lie or steal or commit murder or adultery etc. The negations imply a basic affirmation.

The natural law is an organic complexus of imperatives based upon the value of the human person and the unity of his being. The natural law is, most authentically, the differentiation of man's original nature in the fullness of his being. Until now, however, this law of being has been very poorly articulated. Statements of natural law have been biologistic or psychophysical at most. But this law is really and radically a metaphysical law of being. Today, the natural law is in grave need of metaphysical articulation and rebirth. A new concept of our human nature is required, such that it will become clear to us that there is nothing in the human person that is purely biological in being. Our thinking about human *being* is still very much imbued with animalism. When human reality is interpreted metaphysically, the definition of man as a rational animal, a definition on which the interpretation of natural law has been based, becomes entirely unacceptable and is seen as being destructive to man's awareness of himself. When this definition and its far reaching influences are finally abandoned, our concept of natural law will undergo a radical transformation.

As the natural law has been articulated, wholly based on

justice and not on love, it has required the minimum in moral responsiveness. But as our insight into this great law of being increases or evolves, more and more will be required of us. No longer will we be able to excuse ourselves of evil because of original sin. When metaphysically articulated, natural law is based upon our personal responsibility for receiving our being and for failing to receive our being. Natural law interpreted in this way gives us a really new morality, one that is "ever ancient, ever new," and not just a static dictation or a novelty. The new morality as we have it today, with its emphasis on individual conscience, is partly influenced by 19th century individualism. Combined with an undifferentiated sense of love and situation, individual conscience is readily made to become an escape-mechanism in moral life. *14-8083*

Insofar as situation ethics takes the present situation as if it were the smallest part of an island above the surface of the water, missing the largest and most fundamental part beneath the surface, its judgments are not metaphysically based. A situation is not an atom of space or time, nor is it a private affair. Each situation is an emphasis in a continuum as vast as being. In fact, the original situation of every person and every event is the situation of being. And original sin, the tension between being and nothingness in the universe and in human life, is the first modification of the original situation of being.

Daily situations are very important in moral life. But our interpretation of each situation is as important to morality as the situation itself. If we are going to live a life that affirms being and rises out of nothingness, we need to learn the art of situational interpretation.

Situations are often disturbed and marked by symptoms of moral disease. In order to diagnose the disturbance in the situation, or to recognize its character from its symptoms, the person-in-situation needs to know and to affirm the natural law. Like the medical student who learns to diagnose disease in the light of the laws of human health, we need to know the healthy structures of moral action if we are to interpret our situations adequately. The medical student does not learn about health simply by studying sickness. He needs to study the healthy body so that he may know how to interpret and remedy disease or other disorders.

Another essential part of good situational interpretation is freedom from the feeling of being victimized by situations. This feeling of being victimized is a hangover from the false feeling that we are basically victimized by the original sin of someone else. Every situation in daily life is an existential symbol of the original tension between being and nothingness for which we are personally and socially responsible. If we assume full responsibility for a situation, this will be one important way of responding to the first imperative of moral life, that we receive our being as fully as it is given. In actively receiving the being of a situation, we will not feel victimized by it. Consequently, we will not be too ready to react to a situation by trying to escape from it under the easy name of love or individual conscience. In situation ethics, as we have it today, love is often used as a situational escape-mechanism rather than as a truly creative act.

An example of love that is really being used as an escape-mechanism is cited by Joseph Fletcher, author of *Situation Ethics*. A woman on a Soviet prison-farm wanting to return to her husband and children, and knowing that pregnant women were dismissed, regained union with her family through an adulterous pregnancy. Does love for her family justify her adultery? Joseph Fletcher would give her his "solemn but ready approval" (*Commonweal*, January 14, 1966). But a love that motivates one person to *use* another as a means to escape a situation is in some sense unjust. In the above example, the woman *used* not only a man, but also herself and her child as means to her end. How much was she really motivated by love?

Committing adultery to get out of a prison and return to one's family is normal but unnatural behavior. It is both good and evil. But the good does not excuse the evil. The normal does not excuse and unnatural. The law against adultery is a moral absolute that remains in any situation no matter what the motive or the condition of love.

However, the situationist denies all moral absolutes except "love." But he cannot deny that there are many other kinds of absolutes in life. Anything that exists is a kind of absolute. If it *is*, it is absolutely true that it *is*. It is absolutely true that these letters are on this page. More fundamentally, each person is an absolute in all his experiences, even in being crippled, blind or in a death agony. And each person is a different kind of absolute in a different pattern of life. Why, then, should absolutes be excluded from morality? As the person remains an absolute in any of his experiences, adultery remains adultery in any life situation. There is nothing that can fully justify or excuse this moral evil.

Moral absolutes are like themes in music. And situations are like variations on a theme. The theme of a certain piece of music can be performed in baroque, romantic, classic or jazz styles. Or it can even be slightly varied in its melodic line. Yet the theme remains as an absolute throughout all the variations. As variations include a theme in music, situations include moral absolutes. But the absolute can exist without the situation just as the theme can exist without the variation:

The command to BE is absolute for every one of us, yet it is unique for each of us. It is false to think that absolutes rule out uniqueness. Because there are absolutes in every situation, this does not mean that the same absolute is not also unique in each situation.

Man is the center from which all his situations radiate. And these situations are like the material out of which he creates his life as his most important work of art. One who acts by the first great imperative of moral life, to BE, is ready to receive the being in a situation, and less ready to escape its nothingness. But it is always possible to decide in favor of escape. A desperate situation, together with a lack of personal freedom, is one that partly forgives the reaction of escape. To a certain extent, a woman escaping a prison by means of adultery is forgiven by her desperate situation and her lack of ability to receive that situation. She is partially justified, but in no sense, fully justified.

We should not use a situation as an excuse to act against the law. But if we decide to act against the law in order to escape a situation, we should be ready to recognize that we have decided to do evil, and that though we might be partly justified, we are not fully justified. By trying to fully justify ourselves, we only reinforce in ourselves the original escape from being that is the original sin. We should be ready to forgive ourselves for our evils, but we should refuse to excuse ourselves. Forgiveness implies recognized failure or sin, but an excuse tries to justify failure or sin.

Though the quality of an evil persists in every situation, the degree of that evil differs with situations. A housewife in a comfortable neighborhood who commits adultery to relieve her boredom is in quite a different situation than a woman trying to escape a concentration camp. Though both commit adultery, the degree of evil in their action is modified by the situation. The basic laws of being persist in all situations, but some situations partially forgive evils that other situations do not forgive at all. While partially forgiving, however, no situation excuses an evil. This is true because of our personal responsibility for original sin, or for its effects in our being.

Another example of situational modification in an action that is always morally evil is abortion to save the life of the mother. Due to the advancement of modern medical care, this reason for abortion is virtually outmoded. But if such a case were to arise, a mother who allowed an abortion to save her life would be willing a great evil. Her situation would diminish the magnitude of the evil much more than the situation of a woman who had the murderous operation performed so that she would not be inconvenienced with a child. Even though it might be partly justified by the desperate situation, abortion to save the mother's life is never fully justified. There is another way. "Greater love than this no one has than that by which he lays down his life for one he loves." The mother who would sacrifice her life for her child would rise to the fullness of love. But if she chose the death of her child to escape her situation, her action would be understandable, though not excusable. And this is true because she would be ultimately responsible for the situation and for the evil of the abortion she had chosen. In the tension between being and nothingness, the tension between good and evil must be fully recognized lest we continue to repress our personal responsibility for the original tension in our own being.

The morally creative person actively receives the tension between being and nothingness in his situation, and the tension between love and law. In his act of receiving, the tension becomes creative rather than destructive. He forsakes neither love nor law, but increases his love until it assimilates the law. As the human spirit transcends the human body while remaining fully immanent to the body and not going against it, the spirit of love transcends the law while remaining fully immanent to the law and not going against it.

In the midst of the tension in which we become morally creative, we are evolving beyond the "tree of knowledge of good and evil," and returning to the "tree of life." The natural law, interpreted as our way back to our original nature or fullness of being, does not adapt to social situations and whims of history as much as it it leads us out of the Egypt of slavery to social conditions into the promised land of an ontological or beingful freedom. When Moses led the Hebrews out of the slavery of Egypt, he gave them the law. And this law was not meant to be a new kind of slavery. It was meant to be a way into the promised land, a way into freedom.

The Hebrews valued justice more basically than love, but their sense of justice was already a basic kind of love. Christ brought the fullness of love. But there is no fullness of love where justice is violated. This is why Jesus fulfilled every part of the law. While fully transcending the law, he assimilated its dictates and transformed its spirit.

The natural law, metaphysically interpreted, will lead us out of the Egypt of original sin into the promised land of being. But we are prone to thinking that such a law of being is unrealistic and idealistic. Instead, it is supremely realistic. Man lives not only by bread, comfort and fun, but most of all by meanings and values. Apathy, pleasure without joy, and other escapes from being into nothingness are often thought to be realistic, but these things act as vacuum fillers. True ideals are invitations to reality, and should not be tossed aside as unrealistic.

Today we are witnessing a new growth of moral sensitivity in some areas of response, and a lessening of moral sensitivity in other areas of response. There is a growing readiness to outlaw capital punishment and to condemn war. There is an increasing reaction against cruelty to animals, and a growing awareness of the oppressed. At the same time there is a decreasing attitude of horror toward abortion. In many areas of sexuality, too, there is a lowering of moral sensitivity. The high divorce rates, the spread of Playboyism, pornography, pre-marital and extra-marital sexual involvements, homosexuality, and the continually decreasing sensitivity about contraception are a few symptoms of this insensibility. It seems that periods of extreme sensitivity about sexual morality are also periods of insensitivity in other areas of morality, and vice versa. This dualism is a sign that human sexuality is not well integrated into the totality of human life. Without metaphysical insight and interpretation, we cannot integrate our sexuality into the fullness of our being.

When our sense of morality becomes really new again, and firmly grounded in beingful awareness, we will be able to move into the future of morality by taking full responsibility for our failure to receive the gift of being and gradually overcome the effects of this failure. Jesus showed us that He had the power to dispel all the consequences of the original sin. He cured the sick, raised the dead to life and divided loaves and fish to feed thousands of people in one sitting. He had the power to dispel poverty, sickness and death, but these evils are still very much with us. If we are completely innocent of original sin in ourselves, and if our Savior had the power to free us from its effects, why did He not do so? Perhaps this was the question that tortured Judas. Was he impatient with Jesus, thinking about some way to force Him to use His power to bring the kingdom on this earth now, today? Jesus was put on the spot by Judas, but He did not resort to His power, and died instead. Why? Because we are personally responsible for our own failure to receive our own being and not just innocent victims. Not even our salvation would deprive us of this responsibility.

Chapter 17

NEW DIMENSIONS OF THE NATURAL LAW

If the natural law is meant to lead us out of the Egypt of original sin into the promised land of being, its still hidden dimensions of meaning need to be revealed. A sense of morality that is also a strong and vigorous sense of being entails a more complete revelation of the natural law. But how can we have a new sense of being in morality when we still have so many old ways of thinking? We still think that man's relation with nature is one of master to servant; that animals, plants, earth, air and water are nothing more than means to our ends. Thus, we are in danger of turning the earth into a wasteland.

Though a sense of personalism has changed our view of the natural law, it is still thought that man is basically an animal, and that his faculty of generation is merely biological in nature. We continue to identify things that are not identical, and to separate things that are not separate. A new way of thinking about nature in the light of being is urgently needed in every area of human life and thought.

Man's way of thinking about himself and the world depends both on the first principles of his thought (his sense of being) and on his manner of reasoning from these principles (logic). From its beginning until now, Western thinking has been motivated by an inadequate sense of being, and it has developed through an inadequate logic of identity and separation. Syllogistic reasoning is based upon the identity and the separateness of terms. Thus, the terms of the reasoning process must be univocal; analogical terms invalidate the syllogism.

In the history of thought on sex and procreation, the logic of identity and separation has been very influential. Previously, the coital act was identified with generation; today the coital act and its generative power are thought to be separate in nature. Not long ago, man and woman were thought to have separate roles, and even separate sexual natures, such that any crossing of roles or functions was viewed as being unnatural. But now there is a strong tendency to think that the human nature of men and women is identical, though their biological differences are still admitted.

Both the separation and identification of man and woman are unnatural extremes. Both breed homosexuality. When a person cannot identify with the extreme and separate role imposed upon him by his culture, he tends to identify with his own sex in seeking sexual satisfaction. And when men and women are thought to have the same human nature, there is so little human difference between heterosexual and homosexual relations that the latter seems almost as acceptable as the former. Furthermore, when human sexuality is identified with genitality, men and women who are heterosexual in the privacy of their homes often become "homosexual" when socializing with others. Not having much to share beyond bed, table and children, husbands and wives separate into groups of their own sex for conversation.

In all these examples, identity serves the purpose of separation, and separation supports identity. Where the coital act is identified with procreation, men and women are separated into well-defined roles and functions. A disordered identification with one's own sex leads to a separation from the other sex in homosexuality. And the identification of love with sex results in the separation of sex from procreation. Many of those who practice the internal separation of contraception also identify the natures of man and woman. While they criticize the biologism of sex-for-procreation, they support another form of biologism, that men and women differ only in their anatomy. Still, they say that sex exists for something more than biological reasons.

But how can this be true if sex is nothing more than an anatomical difference between men and women? Without differentiated awareness of the complex unity of human *being*, it is too easy to slip into separations and identities that are not warranted by reality.

It is a very great challenge for the human mind to sustain the paradoxical but true relationship between realities that are neither identical nor separate. The other alternative, difference in unity, is much more complex than identity or separation. But, unless we are able to sustain this more complex alternative, our thinking becomes over-simplifying and erroneous. We need to go beyond the logic of identity and separation, and find another logic, another way of thinking, one that differentiates without reducing things to identities and separations.

In its previous, as well as present, articulation, the natural law is based on short-sighted premises and worked out through a logic of identity and separation. In order to be interpreted in the light of being, the natural law must be viewed in and through a strong sense of being, and worked out through a paradoxical logic of differentiation in unity.

One of the most basic premises of a beingful sense of morality is that of the unity of the world. Such a sense of morality does not begin with the person alone, but with the unity between the person and the rest of the natural world. It is not enough to talk about the person in morality, as contemporary moralists are doing. We must begin to talk about the *being* of the person and his union with the *being* of all that is. The old biologism in morality is superseded by the new personalism, but both must be surpassed by a more authentic sense of being.

In the context of a dynamic sense of the being of the world, the natural law of the person's being, and the laws of cosmological and biological nature, though radically distinct from one another, are also perceived as radically united with one another. The *natural law* and the *laws of nature* are neither identical nor separate. Most thinking about the morality of contraception has been, and continues to be, based on a false identification of the natural law with the laws of nature. In trying to show that the natural law of the person's being, and the laws of biological nature, are not identical, we must be careful not to declare their separation. A declaration of separateness would be just the other side of the error of identification. The laws of nature could not be assimilated into, and transformed by, the natural law in the being of man unless the unity of man is supported by the still more basic unity of man-in-the-world.

Though the natural law resists any kind of essential interference with the personal being of man, it does not resist such an interference with cosmological and biological laws of nature. But this broader interference with nature is still allowed within definite limits. And these limits are part of the natural law. Though man needs to use animals for service and for food, cruelty to animals becomes an unjust encroachment on the rights of being. Through cruelty to animals, a man degrades not only the being of animals, but also his own being. Furthermore, man's technological control of nature is not a limitless prerogative. There is a point where control of the earth becomes sheer rape of the earth. Then, nature itself retaliates and begins to destroy her destroyer. Air and water can hold only so much pollution before man, the polluter, begins to suffer.

The attitude of Western man toward nature is destructive as well as creative. In the contemporary existentialist, Jean-Paul Sartre, the negative side of this attitude toward nature reaches full Manichaean forcefulness. For Sartre, all the things of nature (en soi) are completely separate from human consciousness (pour soi). And the things of nature are viewed as detestable; they must be negated by man's consciousness so that he will not be limited, controlled or determined by anything. When this kind of thinking prevails, what has happened to the creation that "groans and travails in pain" for the freedom of the sons of God? St. Paul was aware of the profound unity of all creation with man, and of the longing in the whole universe for redemption through man's affirmation. But this awareness is gone from Western thought in Sartre. And now, it must be regained anew.

The Sartrian type of freedom is a separation from being. But the rights that man has in and through his freedom are internal to the rights of being, while they are surpassed by the rights of being. Freedom is only one dimension of being. And man's rights through his freedom must be guided by the rights of being. This is the purpose of the natural law. The rights of being exist in man's relation with the world and with himself. There are certain rights of being in animals, for instance, also cruelty to animals is a violation of these rights. Also the right to life that exists in a human person is a right of his very being, one that limits his rights through freedom. Though a person may think he has the right to take his own life, he acts against the rights of his being in doing so. Similarly the rights of being of the human zygote, embryo or fetus in the mother's womb surpass her rights through personal freedom.

Man's hesitation in receiving his own being and the being of the world, is his most basic denial of the law of being, or the natural law. Out of this basic denial of being, all his other failures and negations originate. Even though a person is not aware that some of his attitudes, thoughts, words and forms of behavior are denials of being, he suffers an unconscious anxiety because of them. Man cannot emerge out of the deep anxiety of his being without a growing awareness and affirmation of the law of his being.

Part of this growing awareness of the law of being in man himself is an authentic awareness of good and evil. In and through the logic of identity and separation, good and evil have been treated as extremes that are opposed to each other. The first imperative of the natural law — do good and avoid evil — identifies some forms of behavior with the good and others with evil, and it separates the good from the evil. This separation is reinforced when the good is identified with being and the evil with non-being. In the context of such a separation between the good and the evil, people are forced either to *rationalize* or to *repress* the evil in themselves, rather than authentically admitting this evil. But it is possible to admit the evil in oneself only when it is perceived as being united with the good. The starkly evil, separated from all good, must either be rationalized as being all good, which it is not, or it must be repressed as being totally evil, which again, it is not. In either case, the person fails consciously to *assimilate* the evil *as it is,* and he fails, as a result, to really transform this evil within himself. Rationalization is an attempt to transform, without assimilating, the evil. Thus it is a false transformation that leaves the evil completely unchanged.

Contrary to the traditional way of thinking about good and evil, they are not related as being to non-being. Evil is not just nothingness or a lack of being. It is a *really existing tendency* within being toward nothingness, a tendency not created by God but originated by creatures. Evil is then a kind of being. And all things, insofar as they are being, are good. Though evil is a tendency within being away from itself toward nothingness, it is, as a kind of being, a good. Seen in this way, good and evil are no longer viewed as opposites that are separate from each other. It becomes more possible, then, for the person to admit the evil within himself — the really existing tendency within his being toward nothingness — instead of trying to rationalize it away or repress it out of his consciousness. An authentic awareness of good and evil enables the person to assimilate both within himself, thus increasing his goodness and really transforming the evil so that it may give way to the good.

The traditional way of thinking about good and evil was largely the result of a reaction against Manichaeism. According to the Manichaeans, good and evil are separate substantial

principles of reality. Matter is the evil substance and spirit is
the good substance. St. Augustine and St. Thomas would not
accept the substantial reality of evil, much less its identification
with matter. But in denying the *substantial* reality of evil, and
in calling it a kind of non-being with no real existence at all,
they failed to overcome the Manichaean separation between
good and evil. If the good is being, and if the evil is a kind of
non-being, there is as great a separation between good and
evil as there is between being and non-being.

It is possible to see evil as a kind of being without seeing
it as a *substantial* kind of being. The modifications or qualities
of a substance are just as really being as is the substance itself.
And evil is a *quality of* substantial being. Even the traditional
way of thinking about evil could lead to this conclusion. Evil
was called a privation, and privation was classified as a quality.
But, because being was too strongly identified with substance,
the real being of qualities was not clearly affirmed. In such a
perspective, it was possible to think that the quality of privation is the same as non-being. Certainly, a tendency toward
nothingness right within being is not a substance, but this does
not mean that it is therefore non-being or non-existent. Every
tendency in being exists just as really as the being that is
modified by that tendency. For this reason, evil is an existing
reality, and it must be fully recognized, accepted and assimilated
as such. Otherwise rationalization and repression will continue
to undermine the well-being and moral vigor of man. As long
as these processes are used as escapes from the false separateness of good and evil, people will continue to reinforce in
themselves their basic denial of the natural law of their being.

Chapter 18

CONTRACEPTION AND THE NATURAL LAW

The natural law ethics that has been used to support the traditional intuition of the Church on birth control has been severely challenged, and rightly so! Articulations of the natural law have been based upon an inadequate psychophysical view of human existence. As a result, the natural law ethics has been shortsighted in all its premises.

How is it possible, then, for the traditional ethics to have true conclusions about moral actions when these conclusions are derived from inadequate premises? True conclusions may be drawn from inadequately formulated premises when the real premises are true intuitions that are poorly articulated. In other words, the alleged premises are not necessarily *the* premises from which the conclusions are actually drawn. If the natural law premises, as these have been stated, are inadequate supports for the conclusions of the moral teaching of the Church, what are the adequate sources of this teaching?

The intimate relationship of divine revelation to the metaphysical truth of being fosters in the Church a deeper *sense of being* than she is aware of in her philosophers, theologians and leaders. In the subconscious life of the Church, there is a profound intuition of the unity of being in the human person and of the negation of this unity by certain kinds of human action. For many long centuries, it was intuitively felt and known that contraception is an affront to the sacramental nature of Christian marriage, though the conscious mind of the Church has defended marriage against this practice on the basis of the natural law rather than on the basis of the sacrament. But this natural law, interpreted in a biologistic manner, has only served to undermine, rather than fully support, the values of the sacrament. And the more recent psychologistic interpretation of the natural law, continues to undermine, in a different manner, the same sacramental values. Both the old biologistic, and the contemporary psychologistic, premises of natural law interpretation fall short of the basis of morality in being.

First of all, the old natural law ethics maintained a biologistic stand by defining procreation as the *biological* end of the conjugal act. Contemporary critics certainly have not improved upon this biologism, since they continue to hold that generation is the biological end of the coital act. Where they depart from the previous interpretation of the natural law is in its insistence that intercourse may never be internally separated from its biological end by any means. Contemporaries cannot accept this movement from biological facts to ethical conclusions. And they are right — ethical conclusions are not to be derived from biological premises. But they are wrong in failing to recognize that the generation of human life is no less an interpersonal end of coital intercourse than is the expression of spousal love. The conjugal act does not have a biological end at all. Both of its meanings are radically interpersonal in nature.

The natural law, as the law of being in man himself, does not support a method of reasoning from biological facts to ethical conclusions. Nor does it really support the more contemporary method of reasoning from psycho-personalist facts to ethical conclusions. The conclusions of morality must be derived from ethical, not from biological or personalist premises. And the first principle of the law of being in man himself is the ontological imperative that man receive the unity of his being as it is given to him. This is much more than a biological, or even a personalist, imperative. It is *the* ethical imperative at its best.

The physical organs that participate in a personally chosen action are internally constituted within the ethical dimension of the person's life, not by their biological structure, but by the unity of the person's being. Thus, the physical organs that participate in the act of eating are internally constituted within the ethical dimension of the person's life. But the physical organs that participate in the circulation of blood, though they are fully personal, are not internal to this ethical dimension of life in the same way. This is why gluttony is immoral, whereas high blood pressure is not immoral. And still more importantly, the physical organs that participate in a personally chosen act of communication, whether of conversing or of coital intercourse, are internally present in the ethical dimension of human life. Any internal separation of these physical organs from the personally chosen action in which they are internally constituted is a denial, not so much of the physical structure of these organs, but of the unity of the person's being.

The relationship between the coital act and its generative power is not one that hangs on the person like his clothes, or one that he can put on and take off as he chooses. It is a relationship as deep within him as the unity of his being. By internally separating a chosen action from one of its fully human powers, the person denies nothing less than the unity of his very being.

The rights of being in the human person require the inseparable union of the coital act and its generative power, and these rights of being surpass the rights which the person has over himself through his freedom. Personally chosen actions that deny the rights of being in the human person are much more than physical or psychic evils. Such acts are morally evil.

But it is not enough to recognize that moral evils exist in human life. The whole reality of moral evil must be carefully differentiated in our awareness, since it is complexly differentiated in being.

First of all, there is a difference between moral evil and sin. Every sin is a moral evil, but not every moral evil is necessarily sinful. The person who separates a chosen action from one of its fully human powers performs a moral evil whether he recognizes it as evil or not. If his conscience sincerely fails to recognize this moral evil, his action cannot be branded as sinful. But, if the person is not deeply open to recognizing moral evil in his life, his conscience lacks sincerity. Openness marks sincerity of conscience. A willful closing of conscience may well be sinful.

Some actions, such as walking or running, can become morally evil if done for purposes such as theft or murder. And some actions, such as killing and deceiving, would be morally evil, or would be murder and lying, if done without a justifying purpose. But there are still other actions that can neither be made evil by an evil purpose, nor made justifiable by a good purpose. These actions are evil in themselves regardless of the ultimate purpose for which they are done. They are *always*, or intrinsically, evil actions. Such actions are closer to the essence of original sin than other moral evils; they are explicit denials of the unity of his being by the person himself.

Any internal separation of a personally chosen action from one of its fully human powers, in order to prevent the fruit of that power, is a denial by the person of the unity of his being as it is given to him. Such an action is always morally evil, whether sinful or not. No good, or even apparently necessary, purpose can justify or excuse it.

Still, the human action that is to be regarded as evil in itself must be accurately defined. Not every act of taking what belongs to another is stealing, nor is every act of killing a case of murder. Not every deception is lying. Nor is every use of contraceptives a case of practicing contraception, as was shown in chapter five. Stealing, murder, lying and contraception, as well as other such actions, are always morally evil.

An example of the value of accurate definition in judging the moral status of an action is the differentiation between coitus interruptus and coitus reservatus. Coitus interruptus, or semination after terminating the coital act, is an internal separation of this act from its generative power. But coitus reservatus, the coital act without any semination at all, whether within or apart from the act, cannot be defined as an internal separation of the coital act from its generative power, since the generative power is not involved as it would be if semination took place. Just as the use of contraceptives in the case of rape cannot be defined as an act of contraception because no coital act is involved (copulation is not coitus), the absence of semination in the coital act cannot be defined as an act of contraception because the generative power is not involved. The internal separation of the coital act from its generative power can be realized only when there is a coital act, and only when the generative power is involved by semination.

But it might be wondered whether the coital act without semination is a case of masturbation or not. In order to resolve this question, a definition of masturbation is necessary. Both masturbation and homosexuality are attempts to separate genital stimulation as well as the generative power from heterosexual coital union. These separations are inauthentic forms of human behavior. All willfully induced genital activity is meant to be assimilated into the coital union of man and woman. There is no other way in which this activity can be authentically personalized. Coitus reservatus is not necessarily a case of simple masturbation since it is not as such a separation of genital stimulation from coital union.

Sterilization is an internal separation of the coital act from its generative power; the expression of the generative power, that is, the movement of ova or sperm, is surgically impaired. In male sterilization, the movement of sperm is cut off without interrupting the movement of the fluid that carries the sperm. This seminal fluid is necessary for performing the coital act. Though many people accept the impairment of insemination, they would find any surgical impairment of the coital power entirely unacceptable. In other words, impotence seems more undesirable than sterility. But a surgical impairment of the human power for the coital act is no more seriously deforming than the surgical impairment of the human generative power.

Artificial insemination is another deforming separation. It is a way of activating the generative power apart from the coital act. As contraception is a way of biologizing the generative power in order to prevent conception, artificial insemination is a way of biologizing the generative power in order to induce conception. Such a method of insemination is proportionate only to the strictly biological nature of the reproductive power in animals. If human generation is nothing more than a biological function, there is no reason why human "reproduction" should not be established as a utilitarian department of the government. With the use of enforced sterilization, artificial conception and gestation, it would be very possible for the state to take over this human function. But this could not be done without a massive biologizing, or depersonalizing, of something that is much more than biological in nature. The human generative power is meant to be fully human and intimately interpersonal.

Though the human generative power exists in an inseparable relationship with the power for the coital act, the fruit of this power, the embryo or fetus, might be separated from its natural environment in the uterus and transferred to an artificial gestator in cases where miscarriage or needful surgery would threaten the life of the developing person. Furthermore, the use of artificial gestation would make possible the removal of a defective embryo or fetus for the purpose of correcting the defect. But these would be emergency situations for the sake of saving the life of the embryo or fetus, or for correcting disease or deformity. In any case, such a separation of the embryonic or fetal person from his natural environment would not be comparable to an internal separation of a personally chosen action from one of its fully human powers, as are artificial conception and contraception.

The coital act exists in an inseparable relationship not only with the power to generate new life, but also with the power to love. Just as there is an equality between the two *persons* who share the coital act, there is an equality between the two *powers* of this act. Obviously, the equality of these powers is not based on the frequency involved, since the coital expression of conjugal love is much more frequent than the conceptions that result. Nevertheless, the two powers of the conjugal act — the power to give love and the power to give life — are equal in quality if not in the quantity involved.

The coital act is meant to be assimilated into the power of conjugal love, and the generative power is meant to be assimilated into the power for the coital act. Though the generative power matures before the power for coital union, the human person is not ready for parenthood in early adolescence when his generative organs begin to develop. This earliest maturation must be assimilated into his developing power to love in a conjugal manner before his generative power finds its fully human context. But the principle of assimilation that expresses the particular unity of man's being can be denied in many ways. Every inauthentic separation is such a denial. Just as the coital act can be separated from its generative power, it can be separated from the power to love. Both separations are denials of the very *being* of the coital act, and equally so.

The separation that the person imposes within his being by means of contraception is one that deforms rather than alters his generative power. The use of foam or cream to kill the sperm is an obvious deformation. Other contraceptive deformations may be less obvious, but they are no less real.

Contraception is a direct devaluation of the generative power implying an indirect, but no less real, devaluation of the whole person and the sexual act in which he expresses his being. Since the human generative power is an interpersonal power, one that is activated by two persons together, a devaluation of this power by one of the persons is also a devaluation of this power in the other person, along with an indirect implication regarding the very being of that other person.

Due to the interpersonal nature of the generative power, a physician is not morally justified in requesting semination in order to perform a semen test. Some people cannot see how such a procedure would differ from provoking a vomit for medical examination, something that can be morally allowed. (Cf. G. Egner, *Contraception Vs. Tradition*, Herder and Herder, New York, 1967.) Induced vomiting would be an immoral action if done, as the Romans did it, so that more food might be eaten; the act would then be motivated by gluttony. But masturbation, even for medical purposes, is immediately differentiated from the induced vomit for medical purposes by the fact that voluntary semination involves a power that is essentially interpersonal in nature. The digestive power, on the other hand, is never interpersonal in nature. Furthermore, an induced ejection from the stomach is not a complete prevention of digestion (not all food intake is reversed), whereas masturbation involves the generative power apart from its generative context. If sperm were directly removed from the testicles, or if some sperm were removed from the vagina for medical examination after coitus, both of these procedures would be morally different from masturbation, since the first procedure does not involve the generative power, and the second does not prevent conception. Neither action involves a separation of the generative power from the coital act. Nor is removal of some sperm after coitus comparable to contraception, since this very partial removal does not prevent conception; contraception is intended to be a complete removal of all sperm from access to the ovum.

But it is often supposed that the human person is free to do with his generative power as he chooses. Those who affirm the Sartrian view of freedom will be ready to negate anything other than, or within, themselves that limits their freedom.

Anything that is *en soi* is viewed as separate from the principle of freedom (*pour soi*) and as something that may be negated by the *pour soi*. But this Sartrian view of freedom is based upon an intensely Manichaean philosophy of the world and of the human person in the world. The principle of assimilation based on the radical unity of being in the person is totally foreign to any Sartrian way of thinking.

The exercise of one human act to project an internal separation into another human act is evidence of a person who has taken a stand against the unity of his own being. When this is done by spouses so that they may express their love for each other without an undesirable pregnancy resulting from their action, the denial of the unity of one's own being for the sake of loving another person must be questioned. Contraception is not a matter of sacrificing the unity of one's own being for the sake of love; it is a matter of denying this unity of being. If one person does not receive the unity of his own being in love, how can he receive the being of another person in love?

Insofar as a person devaluates the unity of his own being, he renders himself metaphysically incapable of loving the being of another person honestly, though he may still feel that he is emotionally capable of great love. In order to prevent the emotional disturbance of periodic continence, couples may resort to the metaphysical disturbance of contraception. And though contraception is metaphysically contrary to human dignity and love, spouses seem to remain dignified and loving in spite of it. Many believe that contraception is necessary for them to maintain their dignity and love. But there is a real difference, not a separation, between the psychic and beingful dimensions of human dignity and love. It may be very true that these human values are emotionally possible for some people only at the expense of the beingful dimension of human dignity and love. But if these people are to be honest with themselves they must be ready to admit what they are doing to the unity of their being in order to preserve the emotional unity of their lives together.

Though the practice of contraception is not a case of psychic schizophrenia, it is a kind of metaphysical schizophrenia or ontological neurosis. And, as Carl Jung says in his *Psychology and Religion,* "neurosis is a substitute for legitimate suffering." (Yale University Press, New Haven, 1963, p. 92). Though psychic neurosis is not necessarily due to moral disturbance, the ontological neurosis of denying the unity of one's own being is a moral disorientation. From the point of view of the person's emotional life, contraceptive intercourse may be regarded as normal, understandable behavior. But, from the point of view of the person's being, it is both abnormal and unnatural.

The practice of contraception may be motivated by a selfish purpose, or it may be motivated by a good and apparently necessary purpose. But selfishness does not make contraception morally evil, nor does a good purpose make it morally acceptable. Selfishness and contraception are distinct, though not separate, moral evils; they must be evaluated on different grounds.

Few seem to realize that the anovulant pill, a medical drug, treats marriage as if it were diseased; it addresses the inner sexuality of woman, and even the conjugal act itself, as if these were sources of disease germs. The relatively normal process of ovulation is reduced to an abnormal state. Pregnancy symptoms without pregnancy, as well as blood clotting and other destructive effects, are disorders induced by "science." It is unfortunate that this spurious use of science has been so widely compared to the true science of Galileo.

Acceptance of the anovulant pill along with a rejection of other modes of contraception means that the generative power of woman may be legitimately biologized. This implies a subtle assertion of the inferiority of a woman's sexual nature. In most cases, she is the one who is saddled with the responsibility for contraception. On the other hand, the minimal fertility of woman, when compared with the maximal fertility of man, might suggest superiority in woman, rather than inferiority, to anyone who would care to uphold that point. But quality, rather than quantity, should be the basis of judgment in this matter. The fertility of man and woman, though unequal in quantity, is equal in quality. And the equality in the real sexual difference of man and woman is not undermined by the difference in their degree of fertility. Thus, woman is no more legitimately a contraceptor than is man.

Mechanical contraception (blocking the sperm) and chemical contraception (blocking the ovum), though different in manner, are equal in significance. Justifications for the anovulant have been based on the idea that suppression of ovulation results in a desirable conservation, rather than natural degeneration, of ova. But why conserve the overly abundant? Why conserve the ova while stimulating more freely the expression and degeneration of spermatozoa? To conserve the ova in order to waste more effectively the sperm seems unreasonable.

In his treatment of the existential vacuum which many people experience in the form of apathy and boredom, Viktor Frankl, a Viennese psychiatrist, employs a meaning-theapy in which he tries to help the person find the deeply needed meaning for his existence. Frankl is severely critical of those doctors who give their patients tranquilizers when these people are actually seeking a meaning for their lives. The situation is similar to this when a person goes to his doctor with family problems and is given contraceptive pills. As the question — "what is the meaning of my existence?" cannot be answered with tranquilizers, family problems resulting from a need for emotional and beingful differentiation in sexual life cannot be solved with contraceptives. In both cases, the doctor is satisfied to suppress symptoms without considering their cause. If he is too busy for anything more, he should at least be ready to admit to the patient that he is not solving the real cause of the problem. And he should be able to refer the person to someone else for the help that is really needed.

Before people are able to employ successfully the assimilation method of birth regulation, they need the inspiration of a rich and fulfilling *meaning* for marriage and for the unity of their being in the inseparable relation between the conjugal act and its generative power. But assimilation, the act of receiving one's generative power into his understanding, depends upon meaning for life as well as upon scientific knowledge. Impatience with the method of conception regulation through periodic continence is just one of the many results of a general crisis of meaning in human existence. Ours is an age of profound transition in meaning.

> It is an age of moral bewilderment. For it is only when life as a whole is felt to be meaningful that rules of behavior are felt to be anything more than practical dispositions at the traffic-control level.
>
> (Dom Sebastian Moore, *God is a New Language,* Newman Press, 1967, p. 56.)

Man's ability to assimilate his generative power into his mental life is consonant with his similar, though more spontaneous, ability to assimilate his visual and auditory powers into the conscious acts of observing and listening. The latter can be done without scientific means, but the assimilation of the generative power into personal awareness depends upon a scientific knowledge of ovulation. It would be ideal for people to know exactly when a child might be conceived, or which single coital act would be conceptive. But this implies a similar recognition of those coital acts that would not be conceptive as well.

The idea that it takes many coital acts for generation to take place presupposes that the person does not know the difference between generative and non-generative coital acts. But the possibilities disclosed by science for coming to this knowledge makes the lack of it undesirable — a privation rather than something to be positively proclaimed as a basis for contraception.

The idea that contraception is a way of bringing conscious control into a fertility cycle that is hidden in the darkness of biological processes, completely misses the true meaning of conscious control. The fertility cycle is meant to be assimilated into knowledge so that the real distinction, not a separation, between generative and non-generative coital actions may be affirmed. Both the generative and the non-generative coital acts are natural to man, and proportionate to the unity of his being, except when the potentially generative act is forcefully reduced to a non-generative state. And the human ability to choose acts that are potentially generative, or else to avoid these acts and choose those that are apparently infertile, is also natural to man and proportionate to the unity of his being.

The fact that a woman is fertile only 12-20 hours a month must be significant. Why this minimal fertility? Such a distinction between hours of fertility and the far greater span of infertility must exist, not as an invitation to induced sterility, but as a support of man's need for conception regulation. Infertility is not a separation of a woman's generative power from her being any more than the absence of conscious activity in sleep is a separation of the power for conscious activity from a person's being. A real distinction in being is not a separation, nor does it support a separative treatment. The fact that a woman becomes temporarily infertile at certain intervals does not support the induced temporary sterilization of contraception. And the fact that a woman naturally becomes permanently infertile at a certain age does not support induced permanent sterilization. Death, too, is a process of nature, but the fact of natural death does not support or justify induced death or killing.

It may seem that since the time span of infertility is so much longer than the time span of fertility in a woman, this is actually a basis in nature for reducing fertility to sterility. But the difference in quantity (time span) does not affect the quality of fertility, and gives no authentic indication that the quality of fertility may be deformed by sterilization, whether temporary or permanent. Quality rather than quantity ought to be the basis of judgment in this matter.

The difference between infertility and sterility must be carefully discerned. While infertility, like sleeping, is part of a natural rhythm of life, sterility is a defective condition. Infertility and fertility are related as sleeping and waking, but sterility, like sleeping sickness or being knocked into a coma, is a privation. Whether sterility is congenital, acquired or induced, it is a defective condition. One can take pills to induce sleep in order to encourage or maintain the natural rhythm of sleeping and waking. But sleeping pills used to interrupt this natural rhythm induce a defective condition. Similarly, the same pill can be taken either to encourage and maintain the natural rhythm of fertility and infertility, or to induce a disorder by interrupting this rhythm. If the disorder is induced in order to prevent, rather than to encourage conception, it produces sterility rather than infertility.

The method of conception regulation by periodic continence is based on infertility, but contraception is a temporary sterilization. It is a defective condition willfully induced by the person himself. One who resorts to contraception is not interested in the infertile period, but is concerned only to reduce the fertile state into one of sterility. The act of *assimilating* or receiving the infertile period is radically different from the act of *separating* or destroying the fertile period. Those who deny the difference between the infertility-based method of conception regulation and fertility-based contraception must logically deny the difference between infertility and fertility. But this would be similar to denying the difference between being asleep and awake.

The person who cannot tell the difference between the method that destroys fertility (contraception) and the method that avoids fertility is not well endowed to discern the difference between destroying life by abortion and preventing life by contraception. *As abortion destroys actual life, contraception destroys actual fertility.* But periodic continence, instead of destroying or suppressing fertility, simply avoids it.

The difference between avoiding and destroying or incapacitating should be obvious to everyone. For example, one who avoids a person he does not want to confront does something quite different from destroying that person, or knocking him into a coma, or physically suppressing him in one way or another. Similarly, one who avoids his fertility by periodic continence does something basically different from destroying or knocking out his fertility with contraceptives.

And, though continence and contraception may be employed for the same purpose, for conception control, this same purpose does not reduce them into an identity. A man may rob banks for the money, or hold a responsible job for the money, but the same purpose does not affect the radical difference of these actions.

Even if the method of regulating conception by periodic continence became as simple and effective as contraception, this would not mean that these methods would then have the same effect in human life. The *meaning* of the methods will remain radically different. One personalizes (by assimilation) while the other depersonalizes the human generative power by internal separation. And human beings are more deeply affected by meanings (subconsciously if not consciously) than they are by utilities. In this matter of meaning, "the medium is the message." If both mediums (methods) became equally as effective, the one that works by assimilation would be far less dehumanizing in its immediate and long range effects than the one that works by internal separation.

The widely held view that the marriage as a whole way of life should be procreative, and not any single coital act, such that single acts against generation may be allowed, is one that is based on a false identification of the principle of totality used in medical ethics with the moral life as a whole. In medical ethics, a separation of a diseased organ is allowed in order to preserve the person himself. May the generative power then be separated from individual conjugal acts in order to preserve the good of a whole marriage? Is the totality of a whole span of life the same kind of totality as the being of a person? These are two different kinds of totality. Though the span of a person's life and the unity of his being certainly are not separate realities, they definitely are not the same kind of reality.

To base moral questions upon the marriage as a whole is also to remove the base of morality from the realm of the individual act. This way of thinking about moral questions would apply not only to marriage, but to all other areas of human life as well. No single act, in any area of life, could be judged as morally wrong. Only the way of life as a whole could be judged as morally right or wrong. One might then argue that if a man's moral life as a whole is charitable or *fruitful* in virtue, single acts against this moral fruitfulness, such as hatred, lying or murder, would be allowed. One person may kill another in a single act, yet the morality of that act would have to be judged according to the killer's life as a whole. If his whole life in society cannot be judged as the life of a killer, then his individual act of killing cannot be judged.

Contrary to this way of thinking, there is a principle of totality in every single human action. As the whole person exists in each part of himself, he exists as a whole in each of his actions. Morality is based on the totality of the individual act, and not on the life of the person as a whole. In each of his acts, the person expresses the totality of his being, if not explicitly, then certainly implicitly. This does not mean that individual actions are separate actions, or that morality is based on separate things rather than on something that is total. All the actions of a human life are continuous with one another, inseparable, but really distinct. And each distinct action is a moral unit that neither may be condemned nor justified by the continuum of human actions. A person is individual, but this does not mean that he is separate from other persons; he is meant to be affirmed in his continuity with other persons while retaining his full individuality. Similarly, a human act is individual without being separate from other human actions. The base of morality in the individual act separates it neither from other actions, nor from the person himself, nor from all the actions of his life as a whole.

Contraception, a crude form of self-defense against one's own acts of love, is always morally evil when the coital act is free, even if only minimally so. Where freedom does not exist, as in psychosis or the forceful coercion of rape, the coital act does not exist, though copulation may take place. In such a case, the use of contraceptives induces a physical defect without being a moral evil. However, since psychosis and rape are results of original sin, an indirect moral responsibility is partly present even in these extremes.

Depending upon the extremity of a situation and the degree of actual freedom, the immorality of acts that are intrinsically evil differs in degrees. A situational crisis together with a lack of true sexual freedom qualifies, without negating, the immorality of contraception. Persons who resort to contraception as an escape from a situational crisis ought to be able to forgive without excusing themselves. The "necessary" evil must be acknowledged as the evil that it is. Contraception should not be practiced with complacency, but with a deep moral sadness and regret. Otherwise, the person's responsibility for his deep failure to receive his being is not accepted. Excuses for moral evils are flights from this responsibility. As Maria Montessori said in *The Secret of Childhood* —

> We have an instinctive tendency to mask our sins by protestations of lofty and necessary duties, just as in the war a strip of ground dug with trenches or filled with death-dealing devices was camouflaged as a flowery meadow.

Unless we come to terms with this instinctive tendency to sweep certain things under the rug, or to repress the truth about them, we retard our growth toward the fullness of our being. Unless we are faithful in little things, we cannot be faithful in greater things (Luke 16:10).

Since marriage is one of the closest of human relationships, contraceptive intercourse, morally and metaphysically so similar to lying, is a more serious wrong for spouses who love each other than it is for unmarried persons who do not love each other, but who use sex for entertainment. For these latter persons, the separation of sex from love is the primary evil.

When the desire to avoid conception, and the desire for coital union, seem to conflict with one another, the two inseparable powers of the coital act — the power to express spousal love and the generative power — become similar to the beams of a cross. The generative power seems to cross the desire for a coital union of love. But this is not a time to pull the cross apart. The Gospel imperative, "take up your cross and follow Me," guides and inspires married Christians in the challenge toward growth, with its attendant sufferings, that cannot be authentically avoided.

To show that the equality and inseparability of the conjugal act and its generative power are based on *being* rather than on *biology* has been the abiding theme and purpose of this book. Contraception is a moral negation not because it denies any primary purpose of the conjugal act, but because it denies the unity of the person's being. The previous way of thinking in terms of the primary purpose of the coital act was largely based on biology. But now, in the light of the person's very being, we are able to think in terms of an inseparable equality in the two meanings of the conjugal act. Beyond biologism, and beyond personalism, we encounter the person in his being, and regain the natural law anew.

Pope Paul's encyclical on Human Life has been criticized as promoting a static or fixed concept of human nature and the natural law. But man will not evolve to such an extent that the unity of his being will cease to resist deep forms of separatism. Only if evolution means a movement away from the essential unity of the person's being will contraception be based on evolution. Though some of its articulations may be inadequate or incomplete, Pope Paul's encyclical is a radical call to evolution in love and the freedom that affirms the unity of being — a true change in human nature. For this evolution of freedom all creation expectantly waits.

Our return to the paradise of being is not inevitable. But for redeemed Christians participating in the Resurrection, this return is immanently possible. It can be accomplished. All depends upon our willingness to receive our being and the being of the world. In receiving this gift and grace of being, we become more fully the sons and daughters of God, and the co-creators of the earth.

Appendix

THE EVOLUTION OF LOVE

When Tielhard de Chardin developed the art of reading the contours of the universe, he was not a literalist. His scientific interpretation of the world was not tied to the measurable exteriors and quantities of things. Teilhard was a depth-analyst. Like Freud, who saw the subconscious depth beneath the surface of everyday awareness, Teilhard saw the hidden universe beneath the surface of the everyday world. Both men thought of the deeper reality in terms of psychic energy. For Freud, psychic energy was a basic source of evolution in man's behavior. For Teilhard, it was a basic source of evolution in the whole universe, including man and man's behavior. What Freud accomplished for the science of human behavior, Teilhard accomplished for the science of the universe — a discovery in depth.

Radial energy, according to Teilhard, is the basic energy of cosmic evolution. It is the *within* of everything.[1] Radial energy is a dynamic thrust toward the future completion of creation in the maximum achievement of complexity and centration. Man,

---

1. Teilhard's concept of radial energy is similar to the concept of the **elan vital** or **vital impetus** held by Henri Bergson to be the internal animating force of cosmic evolution. Though Teilhard denied that his thinking was metaphysical, there seems to be a curious similarity between his concept of radial energy and Aristotle's idea that movement and change are results of the desire for God in the world itself (**Metaphysics XII**). Aristotle did not establish the connection of this world-desire for God with primary matter, the principle of potency for movement and change, but this connection seems definitely implied in this thinking. In **Physics I.** he refers to a kind of appetite or desire in matter for form. (Also St. Thomas in **Summa Theol.** I, 5, 3 and **Comm. on Physics I**, 15, 138.) The difference is that

the most complex of evolved beings, is also the most centric or self-aware. Though man emerges at the summit of evolution, the progress of the universe within man himself is unfinished. The thrust of cosmic energy is still projected far ahead of the present human condition toward a new centration in which the great multitude of persons will share a common center of inspiration. This view of radial energy reveals a cosmos with a convergent structure.

But there is another energy which balances the radial tendency toward an ever-increasing complexity by resting in the complexity already achieved. Tangential energy spreads itself out in beings of the same complexity, while, at the same time, binding them together in a specific group. The spreading and binding force of tangential energy accounts for the fact that lower forms of matter remained behind as higher forms evolved. Tangential energy, the externalization of radial energy, is the measurable quantum of the *without* which ordinary science analyzes and manipulates.

The final stage in the cosmic progress of radial energy is the evolution of love. In *The Future of Man*, Teilhard wrote of "a new kind of love, not yet experienced by man, which we must learn to look for."[2] When this cosmic love begins to appear, the minds and hearts of all men will tend to converge toward a common center, Christ, the Omega. Teilhard says, "there is but one possible way in which human elements, innumerably diverse by nature, can love one another; it is by knowing themselves all to be centred upon a single 'super-centre' common to all."[3] This

---

Aristotle did not conceive of the universe as developing by evolution, nor as created by God. For Teilhard, radial energy is the created dynamism of world evolution; it is a thrust of the world toward, Omega, or God. Radial energy might well be described as the internal desire of the world for Omega.

2. **The Future of Man**, Harper and Row, New York, 1964, p. 119.
3. **Ibid.**, p. 75.

love will emerge, not from the tangential energy of the *without*, but from the radial energy of the *within*.

Since the relationship between man and woman is a central source of love in the world, the *within* of radial energy waits upon their relationship for the future evolution of mankind. Until now, the meaning of marriage has been centered largely in the tangential energy of human sexuality, that is, in the spreading of the human group according to the blessing to increase and multiply and fill the earth. But the *within* of radial energy will transform the meaning of this blessing. Man was meant to fill the earth not only tangentially or physically, but also spiritually. This is what St. Paul means when he says that "the eager longing of creation awaits the revelation of the sons of God" (Romans 8:19). This is what Teilhard means when he says that "love is tending, in its fully hominized form, to fulfill a much larger function than the call to reproduction."[4] The whole earth "groans and travails in birth pains" for the love that human persons, in their open awareness, can give. And man's own being groans and travails in pain for the upsurge of the deep, radial energy that is straining in his existence for expression.

> Between man and woman a specific and reciprocal power of sensitization and spiritual fertilization seems in truth to be still slumbering, demanding to be released in an irresistible upsurge toward everything which is truth and beauty.[5]

Where tangential energy is the strongest, in the attraction between man and woman, there the upsurge of radial energy into a new stage of human development will take place. Tangential energy has drawn men and women into physical closeness for the spreading of human elements. But now that the earth is

---

4. **Building the Earth,** Dimension Books, Wilkes-Barre, Pa., 1965, p. 75.
5. **Ibid.,** p. 75.

filled to the point where many are concerned with the problem of over-population, the deeper energy of human sexuality is ready to supersede the externalizing energy, and to bring about not only a new kind of marital diffusion, but also a new kind of sexual love and marital consummation.

The intimacy of "making love" in a genital manner is an expression of the radial-tangential meaning of two in one flesh with a tangential emphasis. Because of the continuity of radial and tangential energy in the human person, the mystical aspect of the deeper sexual force is sometimes felt in the more tangential mode of intercourse. But that which is sometimes, and only momentarily, felt is meant to become continuously more vital. This will mean that the tangential aspect of "making love," *without* to *without* in direct intercourse, will become gradually less necessary, and more free. Husband and wife, in becoming ever more aware of the energy of the *within,* will also become aware that the *within* cannot be most deeply reached through the directness of the *without.* Two people relate interior to interior more deeply and continuously in an indirect way. This is precisely what the nature of radial energy indicates.

The inner radial energy of human sexuality turns man and woman toward the world. They become free to love the world together, and to love one another indirectly, or through the world. For Teilhard, this love for the world means a love for the supreme center of convergence in the universe — the Cosmic Christ. In the being of God-Incarnate, the winds, the waves and the farthermost stars converge, and all are present in the *within* of one another. This cosmic meaning of the Incarnation is intimated by St. John when he says that God's love for the world moved Him to give His only-begotten (John 3:16). Love for the world finds its consummate meaning in the Incarnation. Man and woman, who received together the blessing to fill the world with their communion, need to discover the way of love for the world implied in the Incarnation. When husband and wife so love the world as to give one another to the being of the world, the power of radial energy will have emerged into "the freedom of the glory of the sons of God."

Christ came for the redemption, not only of mankind, but of all creatures. "Go into the whole world," He said, "and preach the gospel to every creature" (Mark 16:16). But no one knows how to tell the good news to the lilies of the field and the birds of the air unless he is imbued with the freedom of the sons of God. Love, the expression of freedom, is the way to tell the good news to the least of beings.

But what is the nature of this love? The word "love" is so freighted with romantic connotations that it sometimes seems bizarre to speak of love as having a cosmic mission, particularly the love between man and woman. Teilhard himself is a thoroughgoing romantic. Even though he is admirably aware of a new kind of love not yet experienced by man, a love that is latent in the cosmic future of radial energy, he is quite incapable of elucidating the quality of this love other than in the manner of Western romanticism. In his *Hymn of the Universe* this romanticism reaches its height.

Rich with the sap of the world, I rise up towards the Spirit whose vesture is the magnificence of the material universe but who smiles at me from far beyond all victories; and, lost in the mystery of the flesh of God, I cannot tell which is the more radiant bliss: to have found the Word and so be able to achieve the mastery of matter, or to have mastered matter and so be able to attain and submit to the light of God.[6]

This passage, and many others, reveals the deepseated romanticism of Teilhard's soul, the spirit of possessing (mastery) and

6. **Hymn of the Universe**, Harper and Row, New York, 1965, p. 27.

of being possessed (submission). But there is another quality of love that is neither possessive toward matter nor "lost in the mystery of the flesh of God." This is a love for the *being* of creatures, rejoicing in them for their own sake; not for the sake of man or for the sake of God. Teilhard continuously speaks of love for material being, but always with the purposes of the scientist and the romantic.

In the Western ethos, matter is either a means to a human end in technological conquest, or it is a stepping stone to God. The nature of that love by which God so loved the world as to give His only-begotten has yet to be revealed through a *conversion of awareness to being*. Even if man had not been in need of redemption, God's love for His creation would have been consummated in the giving of His only-begotten. Love for being is the primordial essence of love.

The world that God loves for the goodness of its being is the world that was given to man and woman together. Created in the image and likeness of God, they were meant to receive the world as it was given, in love for its very existence. Man and woman, so loving the world as to give each other, rise into the fullness of their likeness to God. This is the primordial essence of marriage. Before the nature of this giving-receiving love is discovered and felt, husband and wife will not be able to emerge from the tangential relationship of possessing and being possessed by each other. Neither can receive the world in love for its being unless each is given to the world by the other.

But, in recent times, tangential sexuality is so hyperactive that it seems almost scandalous to talk about the new, radial sexuality waiting to transform the relationship between man and woman. As Jean Guitton says in *L'Amour Humain,*

> Man's sexual need is but slight as compared with his sexual desire, which knows no bounds and makes itself felt

repeatedly at the slightest stimulation. We live in an aphro-
disiac society which multiplies our sexual desires.

Consequently, the contraceptive pills are increased and mul-
tiplied to suppress the procreative effect of this increased sexual
desire. The pills that treat marriage as if it were a disease, mark
the decline of meaning in tangential sexuality itself. Contraception marks a failure of love. And the contraceptive age is a
dark age for Christian marriage.

Referring to the hyperactivity of tangential sexuality, Teilhard
asks, "How much energy do you think is lost to the Spirit of
Earth in one night?"[7] The sin against love, Teilhard says, is the
dissipation in voluptuousness of the energy that is a reserve for
the personalization of the universe. Through this compulsive
wastefulness, "the Earth is continuously dissipating in pure loss
its most miraculous power."[8] If this energy is not conserved by
processes which differentiate the psychic and spiritual powers
for love in the world, the evolution of mankind will be seriously
forestalled. "Love is a sacred reserve of energy, and the very
blood stream of spiritual evolution."[9] This energy ought to be
sublimated or transformed. As the transformation takes place,
Teilhard says, the expression of love between man and woman
will transcend more or less completely that which had been a
necessary organ of propagation.[10] While their love will continue
to be as physical as they themselves are physical, it will gradually
become less functional, or at least, will have less quantification
and more depth-quality in the coital expression of love. "Har-
nessing passion to make it serve the spirit must — on biological
evidence — be a condition of progress. Therefore, sooner or later,

7. **Building the Earth,** p. 48.
8. **Ibid.**
9. **Ibid.,** p. 49.
10. "Esquisse d'un univers personnel." 1936. **Oeuvres.** Editions de Seuil.

despite our incredulity, the world will take that step."[11] What Teilhard calls "the pure feminine," a dimension of sexuality that exists in man as well as in woman, will then have transformed their sexual relationship. The "pure feminine" may be interpreted as the *being* of human sexuality distinguished from the *function* of human sexuality. In the words of Teilhard,

> Man must perceive the universal reality which shines spiritually through the flesh. He will then discover what has so far frustrated and perverted his power to love. Woman is put before him as the attraction and the symbol of the world. He can unite with her only by enlarging himself in turn to the scale of the world. . . . In this sense, Man can reach woman only through the consummation of the universal union.[12]

This is the voice of one crying in the wilderness to prepare the way of love, "the most universal, formidable and mysterious of cosmic energies."[13]

Teilhard, along with Freud, speaks of the sublimation of sexual energy. In his essay on a personalistic universe,[14] Teilhard develops his view on the sublimation of the sexual quantum as a condition for the further evolution of love in the universe. Because of the way in which Teilhard differs from Freud in his interpretation of the nature of psychic energy, his view of sublimation is quite different from that of Freud. For the latter, psychic energy is physiological in nature, and sublimation is an unconscious process of redirecting this energy from bodily goals to higher social, cultural and religious goals. For Teilhard, the

---

11. "L'evolution de la chasteté" (February, 1934), quoted by Claude Cuenot in **Teilhard de Chardin**, Baltimore, Helicon, 1965, p. 29.

12. **Building the Earth**, op. cit., p. 48-9.

13. **Ibid.**, p. 45.

14. "Esquisse d'un univers personnel."

radial component of psychic energy is spiritual in nature, a "spiritual quantum," and sublimation is a conscious process. "Spiritualized Energy is the flower of Cosmic Energy."[15]

Since Teilhard's view of human psychic energy is basically different from that of Freud, his use of the Freudian term "sublimation" needs to be clarified. The Freudian meaning of the term implies a movement from the without to the within, whereas Teilhard's meaning implies a movement from the within to the without, returning again to the within. According to Freud, the unconscious process of sublimation takes place when external social pressures force the individual to substitute higher goals for pleasure goals. This cannot be the meaning of the personalizing process in the context of radial energy. Instead the energy of the within draws into itself (assimilates) the energy of the without. This internalization of tangential energy is also a transformation of tangential behavior. Physical closeness between husband and wife becomes more and more internalized. The radial *being* of the body gradually supersedes the externalizing *function* of tangential intercourse. Husband and wife then experience the intimacy of *being* love without necessarily, and therefore freely, *making* love in a genital manner.

In the present state of hyperactive tangential sexuality, the intimacy of husband and wife often is compulsively functional. However, as radial sexuality emerges in the human community, the age-old compulsion will become obsolete. Chastity will become man's way of life, not because he will have become less sexual, but because he will have become increasingly more sexual. Internalized sexuality is an increase, rather than a loss, of sexual life; it is the very promise for the evolution of human sexual being.

Radial energy is a dynamic world-continuum, the cosmic within, which all creatures share despite their many differences.

---

15. **Building the Earth**, p. 71.

This innermost dynamism of the world reaches its most splendored revelation in the relationship between man and woman to whom the whole world was given in the beginning. This is the world-meaning of original sin, that man and woman lost the *within* of the universe, the beingful ground of all creatures, and losing the radial interiority of beings in the world, they lost their radial interiority within each other. This loss of *within*ness resulted in their tangential clinging to each other, possessing and being possessed, a desperate attempt to compensate for their lack of interiority with each other.

But that which was lost is being regained. Communion and the cosmic friendship between man and woman, "more active than all active things," is beginning to be born out of the birth-travailing of the created universe. The flowering of the radial upsurge of human sexuality in a communion of love for the being of the world is beginning in our time. Through the radial love between man and woman, both in marriage and in celibacy, the transfiguration of Tabor is meant to extend into the whole world, increasing and multiplying and filling the earth. Then, the words from Tabor will resound with cosmic meaning; man and woman will say once again, as they said before they lost their own being and the being of the universe, "It is good for us to be here."

— Reprinted with permission from **Insight**, Winter, 1968, pp. 11-14, Mary R. Joyce.

INDEX

THE PROMISE TO LOVE
Wilfrid J. Harrington, O.P.

Before we can understand the role of the laity we must first regain a fuller appreciation of the sanctity of married life in all its dimensions. Until recently, Christian marriage received scant attention from theologians; it was a subject relegated, for the most part, to canonists whose complex of laws and moral strictures gave us a very inadequate, dreary and negative view of the way of life in which most of the People of God find their salvation.

Happily times have changed; and today — more than any other time in the history of the Church — we are placing first things first and seeking a new understanding of the sublimity and sanctity of congugal love.

THE PROMISE TO LOVE — (the author's wedding gift to two young friends) — presents a splendid insight into the scriptural teaching on marriage. It will help married couples to deepen their appreciation of life together and will certainly inspire those on the threshold of marriage.

Only an expert exegete could have handled the subject with such understanding, finesse and clarity. This is a book to recommend.

$2.95

CHALLENGES OF LIFE
Ignace Lepp

This provactive and thoughtful study of man as he is today is based on the data of scientific experience.

The great themes which occur again and again in modern art and literature are illumnatingly presented. Adventure and risk, freedom and responsibility, the meaning of vocation, the call to growth, the need to keep responsive and openminded toward life, all these are discussed vigorously and clearly.

The author boldly faces up to the basic question of the very possibility of making a free choice, of being committed. Is man merely conditioned and determined? Can he raise above his situation whilst yet remaining in it? Is all this what can be said about sin, about fear, unrest, anxiety?

"This is a book that offers an intense insightful vision of life as an unending series of challenges by which man must grope his way toward God. It manages to communicate hope and enthusiasm for living, as well as the spiritual stimulation of listening to a truly wise, sensitive and optimistic human being . . . a rare piece of writing that has our unreserved recommendation." *The Register*

Book Club of the Month Selection—Sister's Book League, Thomas More Assoc.

$4.95

THE MYSTERY OF JESUS
Pierre R. Bernard, O.P.

"Among you stands one whom you do not know" (John 1:26). This meditative study of the personality of Jesus is a masterpiece of prayerful scholarship — the fruit of a lifetime of careful research. It is based on the four Gospels, and leads to a more intimate understanding of Christ the Lord.

"THE MYSTERY OF JESUS takes the reader beyond the mere narrative of eternal events into the very heart, mind and soul of our divine Lord, showing us both the reality of his divinity and humanity.... It is a true masterpiece and deserves to be a bestseller, as evidenced by the acclaim it has received in its French, Spanish, Italian, German and Portuguese editions." REV. JOHN A. O'BRIEN, NOTRE DAME

"The most perfect commentary of modern times. It holds the reader spellbound. This is a book I would have loved writing myself, developing the same theme, using the same style." JEAN GUITTON

"A work which is worth a whole library. Its equal may not appear in the next five years." PANORAMA CHRETIEN

2 Volumes $15.00

BE SONS OF YOUR FATHER
Peter J. Riga

It is most opportune that the wonderful insights of modern exegesis on the structure and content of the text of our Lord's Sermon on the Mount should be presented in such a lucid and popular way. The Sermon tells us what Christian life and morality are all about ... and there are few other places in the Bible where the contrast and difference between the law of the Old Testament and the New become so abundantly clear.

As recounted by Matthew and, in a shorter version by Luke, the Sermon on the Mount focuses our attention on the primacy of love. The decalogue, which seems too negative and impersonal in approach, is transformed on the mountain of the beatitudes. We are no longer to walk in fear: the God of love is our father ... and we are the chosen children who were born to inherit the joy of abounding life which surpasses the hopes and dreams of mortal man.

Father Riga writes with an enthusiastic clarity. In analyzing the structure, literary form and particularly, the message and purpose of the Sermon, he shows his keen awareness of modern biblical scholarship. But above all he shows a deep concern for a new view of the Good News of Jesus — a view which has all too often been clouded by an inadequate catechesis and a theology more consonant with the Old Testament than the New.

At a time when the word "renewal" is in danger of losing its fuller meaning, this concise book will enable us to rediscover its import ... to shed our inherited misconceptions of Christian life and morality — and to see the splendor and challenge of Christ's invitation: *Come follow me.*

$3.95

SEX, FERTILITY & THE CATHOLIC
Donald and Helen Kanabay

The trouble with most books on rhythm is that they either bore the reader or scare him way. In our attempt to reach a large audience with our message — that the rhythm method is not only an efficient means of controlling births, but is also an efficacious means to sanctity in Christian marriage — we have employed an approach that is, to say the least, unorthodox, and is liable to objection from some quarters that the authors have been 'indelicate.'

But on the other hand we believe that desperate circumstances require unusual remedies, and that the average couple attempting to practice rhythm is fast approaching the point of desperation. That's our windup. Here comes the pitch.

ppr. $1.50